There was an Old Man with a beard, who said, "It is just as I feared!—
Two Owls and a Hen, four Larks and a Wren,
Have all built their nests in my beard."

There was an Old Man who said, "How—shall I flee from this horrible Cow;
I will sit on this stile, and continue to smile,
Which may soften the heart of that Cow."

CHRISTIE'S REVIEW OF THE SEASON 1979

Underglaze copper-red
and white Ming
wine jar
Middle to third
quarter of the 14th
century
18½ in. (47 cm)
high; 17¼ in. (44 cm)
diameter
Sold 9.7.79 in London
for £95,000 ($209,000)
Sold on behalf of the
Gorhambury Estates
Company

CHRISTIE'S REVIEW OF THE SEASON 1979

Edited by John Herbert

STUDIO VISTA · LONDON

A Studio Vista book published by
Cassell Ltd.
35 Red Lion Square, London WC1R 4SG
and at Sydney, Auckland, Toronto, Johannesburg,
an affiliate of
Macmillan Publishing Co., Inc.,
New York.

First published 1979
Copyright © Christie, Manson & Woods 1979

Design and layout:
Norman Ball/Logos Design, Datchet, Berkshire
ISBN 0 289 70911 3

Printed in Great Britain by Sackville Press Billericay Ltd,
Billericay, Essex, and bound by
Webb Son & Co. Ltd, Ferndale, Glamorgan

Endpapers:
Eight of the 49 pen and ink drawings from the autograph
manuscript of Edward Lear's *The Book of Nonsense* which sold
for £9,500 ($19,655) and was part of the Houghton Library

**The currency equivalents given throughout the book are based on the rate of exchange
ruling at the time of the sale. Any apparent contradictions are due to fluctuations in the
exchange rates during the course of the season**

CONTENTS

Mottled apple and
emerald-green jade
pendant
1 ¾ in. (4.6 cm) long
Sold 11.7.79 in
London for £10,000
($22,100)

Mr John Lumley selling Ferdinand Hodler's *Thunersee von Leissigen aus* for a record £295,000 ($646,050) in the Mettler Collection of Impressionist and Post-Impressionist paintings on 2 July, which totalled £2,625,000 ($5,749,845)

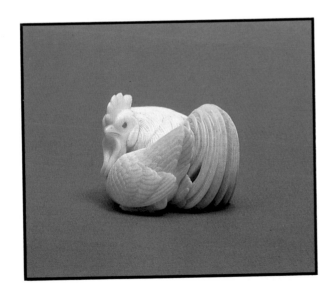

Ivory netsuke of a cockerel and a hen
Signed Kaigyokusai koku, with seal
Masatsugu
Late 19th century
Sold 6.3.79 in London for £19,000
($38,000)
Record auction price for a netsuke

A

CATALOGUE

Of the genuine, rich and very extensive

WARDROBE,

CONSISTING OF A GREAT

Variety of Masquerade Dresses,

THE PROPERTY OF

Mr. *SPILSBURY*,

Late of TAVISTOCK STREET,

Retired from Business;

WHICH WILL BE SOLD BY AUCTION,

By Mess. Christie and Ansell,

At their Great Room,

THE ROYAL ACADEMY, PALL MALL,

On THURSDAY, FEBRUARY 4, 1779,

AND THE FOLLOWING DAY.

To be viewed till the Sale, which will begin at
Twelve o'Clock.

Catalogues may be had at the Place of Sale, and at Mess.
Christie and Ansell's, Pall Mall.

CATALOGUE

OF

THE FIRST PORTION

OF THE

VALUABLE STOCK

OF

MR. MARKS,

OF OXFORD STREET,

WHO IS RETIRING FROM BUSINESS;

Comprising Oriental, Sèvres, Dresden, and English Porcelain; Chinese
Enamels, Carvings in Jade, Arms, Metalwork, French Clocks and
Candelabra, Handsome Ivory Tankards, Gold and other Snuffboxes,
Bijouterie, Limoges Enamels, and a large number of other Decorative
Objects:

WHICH

Will be Sold by Auction, by

MESSRS. CHRISTIE, MANSON & WOODS,

AT THEIR GREAT ROOMS,

8, KING STREET, ST. JAMES'S SQUARE,

On WEDNESDAY, FEBRUARY 5, 1879,

And Two following Days,

AT ONE O'CLOCK PRECISELY.

May be viewed Two Days preceding, and Catalogues had, at
Messrs. Christie, Manson and Woods' Offices, 8, King Street, St.
James's Square, S.W.

Books and Manuscripts

from the Library of

Arthur A. Houghton, Jnr.

Part 1: A-L

which will be sold at Auction by

CHRISTIE, MANSON & WOODS LTD.

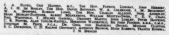

Consultants: I. O. CHANCE, C.B.E.   A. G. GRIMWADE

at their Great Rooms

8 King Street, St. James's, London, SW1Y 6QT

Telephone: 01-839 9060.   Telex: 916429   Telegrams: Christiart, London, S.W.1

On Wednesday, June 13, 1979, at 11 a.m.

and

Thursday, June 14, 1979 at 11 a.m.

*MAY BE VIEWED THURSDAY, FRIDAY, MONDAY
AND TUESDAY PRECEDING*

Illustrated Catalogue, (48 plates, 6 in colour) Price £6.00

In sending Commissions or making enquiries, this sale should be referred to as
ARISTOTLE

1779 — 1879 — 1979

ARTHUR GRIMWADE

'Will you write something for this year's Review?' asked the Chairman. 'But I did so in 1972 to celebrate my fortieth Christie's birthday.' 'Well, perhaps you'll think it over.' So I did and it occurred to me that it might be an interesting exercise to go back one and two centuries from today and see what we were up to in 1879 and 1779 and the contrasts that emerged between those particular two 'thens' and now.

In 1779 James Christie was 49 and had been running his own business since at least 1766. His Pall Mall neighbour Gainsborough had painted the well-known portrait of him the year before — an example surely of the closest rapport between warm friends and the relaxed assuredness of a leading figure of the London art world of the day. He was no longer working entirely alone, having taken as a partner the shadowy Ansell whose name remained in the catalogues until 1784 but of whom little seems to be known. A great storm ushered in the new year. Damage was done all over the country and even the trees in St James's Park close behind the Great Rooms in Pall Mall were uprooted. Three weeks later Christie lost a close acquaintance of his circle with the death of David Garrick and was perhaps not feeling at his happiest when he took the first sale of the year on 22 January with 'A Capital well-chosen Collection of Pictures of a gentleman brought from his Villa at Putney' — a two-day sale which, with 'A Superb Crane Neck Coach' and 'A Do. Chariot' written in at the end of the catalogue, totalled £408.17.0.

Next week he was selling the contents of a house in Hertford Street and it is clear that London house sales were a frequent event, the catalogues presenting tantalizing glimpses of elegantly furnished rooms, rather contrary to the impression one sometimes gets from the settings of conversation pictures of the day. These and picture sales were staple fare, but Christie was full of surprises as when in February he offered the Masquerade wardrobe of the Costumier Spilsbury, foreshadowing the amazing interest taken in the Chanel Sale this season. In 1779 you could have had lot 29, 'Mother Shipton, with Point ruff and cap, mask and stick', for 15 shillings and 6d, or 'A Lady's most expensive rich sattin dress, black vest and train . . . quite new' for £5.17.0, apparently the top price of the sale. A far cry indeed from Chanel's beige tweed suit at £2,400 ($4,800) last December.

The year was to bring a total of 89 separately catalogued sales, many of several days' duration, producing a total of 212 days on which the hammer was wielded, and included some fascinating events; as, for example, on 3 March, 'Part of the Stock of James Cox, A Bankrupt' who was, of course, the Fabergé of the London of his day — a sale of only 18 lots but producing four of the highest-priced lots Christie sold that year, such as 'A sword hilt of the Turky blue enamel enrich'd with valuable brilliants, emblems and trophies of war magnificently

Portrait of our founder James Christie by
Thomas Gainsborough, RA
(This has been for many years in the J. Paul
Getty Museum, Malibu, California)

displayed with infinite taste' which sold for 312 guineas, while 'A ditto equally superb' bettered its claim to equality by going to 425 guineas and a third and fourth produced 317 and 635 guineas respectively. What is the equivalent of these sums today? Three days later the descent from the sublime to the ridiculous was made with the offering of 'all the valuable materials of the Spacious Conservatory, Hot Houses, Succession Houses, Stores &c. of A. Robinson Bowes, Esq. at his villa in the King's Road, Chelsea' for a total of £876.6.0. We can scarcely parallel that today or, alas, the sale of 'the genuine Household Furniture, Ten Bay Coach Geldings, A Saddle Mare, Eight Road Horses and Mares, A Coach, Three Post-Chaises, Harness and other Implements of Mr. Boulden at the Black Horse Livery Stables on the West-Side of the Haymarket' on the previous 18 February, its best price a 'Bay nag tail Saddle mare' at 12 guineas — unless we call into balance the spectacular Car Sale in Los Angeles on 25 February last in which Patrick Lindsay sold the 1936 Mercedes-Benz 500K Roadster for $400,000 (£210,526).

We certainly did our best in 1779 insofar as books and music were concerned with the offering for three days in April of 'the Truly Valuable and Curious Library of Music, late in the possession of William Boyce, Organist and Composer to his Majesty . . . Consisting of all Dr. Green's Curious and Valuable Manuscripts . . .'. Christie certainly knew how (if the play on words be pardoned) to pull all the stops out on such an occasion! In spite of his enthusiasm, however, the top price in the sale was for 'A most capital Violincello finely preserved, by Antonius Stradivarius of Cremona, the signature of the Maker in his own Hand-writing with the year 1700' at 30½ guineas. It is entertaining to speculate what those present at this sale would have thought of the excitement of the sale of the Wagner Manuscripts in New York last October for the remarkable total of $1,376,807 (£688,403), or in a wider but purely English

Mr Seijiro Matsuoka, a Japanese museum owner in Tokyo, admiring the 14th-century underglaze copper-red and white wine jar which he had just purchased for £95,000 ($209,000). This wine jar was discovered by Sir John Figgess, Christie's Oriental Ceramics Director, in one of the cloakrooms at Gorhambury, Hertfordshire, the home of the Earl and Countess of Verulam. Only five other examples would appear to be recorded

vein the competition that took the books offered in Part I of the Arthur Houghton Library to a total of over £1,500,000 (which, as the pound continues to improve, means a U.S. equivalent of $3,421,000).

Of more aesthetic interest to collectors of today must be the sale on 5 May and three days following of 'the Remainder of the Valuable Stock of the Chelsea Porcelain Manufactory . . . without reserve (the Lease of the Premises being expired)', a matter of 416 lots which totalled £807.4.6 and produced a top price of 21 guineas for 'a very complete Table Service, Dresden pattern' of 96 plates, 23 dishes, a pair of soup tureens, a pair of sauce tureens and three pairs of sauceboats; or to students of English drawings the event of 11 June which included a number of James Thornhill's drawings for Greenwich Hospital.

And so we might go on but enough has been said, I hope, to show that two centuries ago the establishment was just as unequalled as now for offering to the gaze and prospective purchase of all and sundry an infinite variety of acquisitions. What for instance did 'A fashionable Crane-neck Vis-a-Vis painted a Devonshire brown' look like, which fetched 33 guineas in a house sale in Upper Grosvenor Street in October 1779? And what today would South Kensington make of the sale of 'Mr. Insley, Sedan Chair Maker, Turner and Toyman bankrupt in Mary-la-bonne Street, Golden Square' with '10 Sedan Chairs offered in Succession', or the toys which included 'a Kitchen furnished, ditto unfurnished, a tree climber, two drummers, chair and men, a fountain and a farm yard', all of them in one lot knocked down for 16s 6d. One hazards a guess that if these had survived till today they would be the star turns illustrated in one of Susie Mayor's fascinating sales at Christie's South Kensington.

Prices in 1779, of course, are virtually meaningless to us today and since unfortunately many of the sales, although with each lot price entered, are untotalled, there seemed little to be gained by a complicated attempt to procure a total for the year. But we are on more established ground when we turn to 1879, where the sale catalogues are meticulously maintained and totalled, as, indeed, the only legal record of an otherwise verbal or even visual transaction of bidding. Here I can record that 110 sales entailed 151 days of selling in the year to produce a sold total overall of £389,600, or slightly less than *La Grande Loge* by Toulouse-Lautrec, from the virtually unknown Mettler Collection of Impressionists from Switzerland, realized with premium on 2 July. Against this Victorian total of well less than half a million, we have to set our total for world-wide sales for 1978-9 of £110,358,000 ($255,000,000), to which New York contributed £29 million ($58 million).

We have by 1879 some reasonable possibility of comparing prices, provided always, of course, that we realize we are counting gold sovereigns then as against the 'wallpaper' of today, and some intriguing parallels can be discovered. By the year in question the market for Modern Pictures of the day (by which our predecessors meant indeed those that had been painted sometimes only a few years before) had become probably the most important branch of the King Street sales.

There were fifteen such sales in 1879 in rapid succession, three in February, two in March, three in April, the first carefully announced, to forestall, no doubt, any suggestion that the vendor was financially straitened, as the property of Colonel Barrows 'who in consequence of ill-health has now determined to let his residence in Worcestershire', and some seven more of the same class later in the year. In the sale of Joseph Arden's collection it is interesting to find J. F. Lewis's watercolour of *The Harem of a Memlook Bey*, painted for the deceased owner in 1850, fetching 690 guineas (£724.10), a good if not exceptional figure for the day but still a rather faint foreshadowing of the extraordinary reception of the same artist's *Intercepted Correspondence* last May when it realized £220,000 ($440,000), a record auction figure for any Victorian picture, let alone for this particular artist. On 24 June of the Victorian season a drawing by Turner of Cologne was bought-in for 400 guineas, but, since no size or description is given, one cannot say whether it was either of the two which have been sold this last season for £9,500 ($17,820) and £22,000 ($44,000) respectively. What we do know at least is that the former came from the collection of William Leech in 1887 — eight years later than 1879 — when it cost 120 guineas.

One of the best of the 1879 sales of applied art was that for the Earl of Lonsdale in March, which offered a mixed menu of 'Fine Pictures, a large collection of Old Porcelain and Decorative Objects'. The star turn in the porcelain was a Sèvres Rose-du-Barri Cabinet at 805 guineas, while 'A Fine Square shaped Chelsea vase, deep blue ground with four large medallions of Chinese figures . . . and exotic birds' made 540 guineas, which must have caused a flutter in the china-collecting world of the day. The French furniture, alas so tantalizingly underdescribed and unattributed, included a Louis XIV Buhl library table at 400 guineas bought by that king of Victorian applied-art dealers Wertheimer, who also acquired a pair of Buhl pedestals at 620 guineas. The Earl's 583 lots in three days totalled £19,336.17.6, the shillings and pence, of course, the result of bids in half-guinea stages for minor lots.

In surveying that year's business one is left with the impression that the art market moved then in a comparatively restricted field in which, as has just been said, relatively new pictures and drawings bulked largely, to be followed by fine furniture, Oriental and European porcelain, some — but not much — silver (the strong rooms of the peerage were not yet being

Mr Kazuo Fujii,
President of the Fujii
Gallery, looking at *The
Lady from the Sea* by
Edvard Munch, after
paying £155,000
($339,450) for it

plundered to satisfy death duties) and very little jewellery, probably because those in need sold for cash or even resorted to the pawnbroker with hopes of later reclamation. Japanese lacquer made an occasional appearance, and a few book sales and three wine sales round off the picture.

What a contrast today. Not only of course is King Street the mother church of a rapidly growing and extraordinarily healthy network of young daughter establishments with their own incumbents-in-charge (to prolong the ecclesiastical vein) — seven new European representatives appointed this year, a second saleroom opened in New York on South Kensington lines and the purchase of Edmiston's Glasgow to provide auctioneering activities north of the Tweed. But the expansion of markets is something of which our Georgian and Victorian predecessors could never have dreamt. 'Heathen gods' from the Pacific or tropical Africa, a Torres Straits turtleshell mask, Nepalese bronzes, early photographs like the Edward Weston 'Shell' sold in New York in May last for $9,500 (£4,750), Tiffany lamps like the spider-web mosaic and bronze example at $150,000 (£75,000), Elizabethan glass like the Richard Grenhal Verzelini goblet with its glued-together foot at £75,000 ($142,000), the 14th-century Ying Ching wine ewer with its 'thick and brilliant very pale blue glaze' or perhaps the winner of this year's 'Prize for Purity', the Yung Lo white glazed stem-cup sold by Mr Shue Chi Lau for £40,000 ($76,000) last December.

Or the human touch of Elizabeth Browning's rough working notes in the wonderful first part of the Houghton Book Collection, the excitement of the sale of Matisse's *Le Jeune Marin I* for the world record price of £720,000 ($1,576,800), the rare Elizabethan silver casket of 1589 never before recorded, or the ridiculous gold and enamel caterpillar automaton in the Geneva sale 'advancing on three wheels in a naturalistic manner' as we catalogued it, or as perhaps our Georgian predecessors might have said, 'admirably constructed to move as to the life'. Turn the pages and choose your fancy. I guarantee you will not be bored.

Negotiated Sales

CHRISTOPHER R. PONTER, LL.B.

During the past eighteen months when the role of the National Land Fund in helping to preserve the heritage has been the subject of great public debate, it is satisfying to record that Christie's have utilized the existing procedures to negotiate a number of private treaty sales of important works of art — either direct to public collections or to the Treasury in lieu of death duties.

In the early part of 1977, we were instructed to sell Giovanni Bellini's *Madonna and Child Enthroned* and in view of the significant tax advantages available, we advised that an approach should be made to the Birmingham Museum and Art Gallery, where the painting had been on loan since 1967. Although valued at over £1 million ($2,100,000) in the open market, the net acquisition price to the museum was agreed at £400,000 ($840,000), and following a strenuous national appeal, we were pleased to learn that their efforts had been successful in retaining this masterpiece for Birmingham (see illustration opposite).

Whilst great publicity has been given to the continuing sale at auction of the remaining parts of the Hooper Collection of ethnographica, we advised the administrators of the estate that certain items were of such 'pre-eminent interest' that they should be offered to the Treasury in lieu of tax. These included a superb Tlingit frontlet headdress, carved as a bear with frog on chest (7 in. (18 cm) high), sent to England by George Hills, first Bishop of Columbia. Worn by persons of rank on ceremonial occasions, 'the top of the headdress is filled with eagle or other birds' down, which falls like snow in the motions of the dance'. This headdress was allocated to the Royal Scottish Museum. A fine Haida oil bowl of mountain sheep horn, carved in relief as a shark (7½ in. (19 cm) long), and a rare 16th/17th-century Brazilian wood carving, probably a snuff-tray (see illustration on p.18) from the Lower Rio Tapajos area were allocated to the British Museum.

During the course of administering an estate in Cumbria we were asked to offer and negotiate the transfer to the Treasury of a little-known but important group of paintings and drawings by Charles Towne valued at £200,000 ($420,000). Negotiations proved successful, and in deference to the late owner's wishes the collection was ultimately allocated to the Walker Art Gallery, Liverpool, an area with a strong local association with that artist.

Again, from the estate of the late Baron Hatvany, we negotiated the sale to the Treasury of three pictures where the 'tax credit' complemented the results of the sales through the auction room to achieve a very satisfactory net benefit to the estate. The pictures accepted comprised an important panel by Sir Peter Paul Rubens, *Jacob and Esau* (19 × 15½ in. (48 × 39.5 cm)); a *Madonna and Child* by Giovanni Bellini (on panel — 37 × 23¼ in. (94 × 61.5 cm)), and a fine example of a drawing by Francesco di Giorgio, *Adam and Eve* (see illustration on p.16).

Opposite:
GIOVANNI BELLINI: *Madonna and Child Enthroned, with Saints and a Donor*
Signed and dated 1505, on panel
Acquired by Samuel Woodburn for 41 guineas in a Christie's sale of 1812, it later belonged to the East Anglian collector Dawson Turner
Following the disposal of his collection through Christie's in 1852, it was sold to Nieuwenhuis for 360 guineas, but by 1878 this altarpiece was hanging in Ashburnham House
It was later acquired in 1899 by Vernon J. Watney of Cornbury Park, and thence by descent
Now in the Birmingham Museum and Art Gallery

14

FRANCESCO DI
GIORGIO: *Adam and
Eve*
Pen and brown ink
13 × 10 in.
(33.2 × 25.3 cm)
Formerly in the
collection of William
Holman Hunt, by
whom it was
purchased in Florence
1867; acquired
through Christie's
4 December 1964
by the late Baron
Hatvany, from whose
estate it was accepted
by the Treasury

ALFRED SISLEY: *Rue de Village*
Oil, 17 × 22 in. (43.2 × 56 cm)
An attractive example of the artist's work of about 1874
Accepted by the Treasury from the estate of the late Mrs M. C. Honeyman

We are also pleased that we were able to secure the transfer to the Fitzwilliam Museum, via the Treasury, of one of the very few drawings known to be by the Venetian painter Vittore Carpaccio. This drawing shows two groups of ecclesiastics facing one another, and is in pen over a preliminary sketch in red chalk; it measures 8¾ × 10¾ in. (28.3 × 27.3 cm). In the 18th century it belonged successively to the English painters Thomas Hudson and Sir Joshua Reynolds, PRA; in the 19th century to Sir E. J. Poynter, PRA; and in the 20th century to the Earls of Harewood.

Important and rare Brazilian wood carving, probably a snuff-tray
The handle formed as a standing female with a jaguar crouched upon her back
Lower Rio Tapajos/lower Rio Trombetas area
16th/17th century
12½ in. (31.8 cm) long
Allocated to the British Museum following acceptance by Treasury

Elsewhere mention is made of the successful launching of our new venture in Glasgow with a group of pictures of Scottish interest derived from the Wemyss Honeyman Collection. That estate also included a number of important Impressionist pictures, and again it was our advice that two paintings by Alfred Sisley were of pre-eminent interest: *Rue de Village* (*c.* 1874; see illustration on p.17) and *L'Eglise de Moiet* (*c.* 1893: 20 × 32 cm. (51 × 81 cm)). These have been accepted by the Treasury in lieu of death duties, but as yet have not been allocated to any particular gallery.

PICTURES, DRAWINGS
AND PRINTS

PIETRO DA RIMINI: *Triptych: the Resurrection; the Birth of Christ, the Annunciation to the Shepherds and the Journey of the Magi; and Noli Me Tangere*
On tooled gold-ground panels
Central panel 7 × 7¾ in. (17.7 × 19.8 cm)
Wings 7 × 3¾ in. (17.7 × 9.6 cm)
Sold 1.12.78 in London for £65,000 ($123,500)
From the collection of G. H. Dixon, Esq.

These unpublished panels, which may originally have formed part of a larger complex, are notable additions to the work of Pietro da Rimini, one of the most refined masters of the 14th-century school of Rimini

GIOVANNI DI PAOLO: *Scene from the Life of Saint Ansanus*
Predella panel
9¾ × 13¾ in. (24.9 × 35.2 cm)
Sold 29.6.79 in London for £80,000 ($168,000)
Formerly thought to represent the Martyrdom of Saint John the Evangelist, this belongs, as Professor Kaftal recognized, to a
predella of scenes from the life of Saint Ansanus, panels from which are in the Bargello at Florence and at Esztergom

FRANCESCO PESELLO, called PESELLINO:
Madonna and Child with Saint Julian, Saint Francis and two Angels
On panel
29¼ × 19 in. (74.3 × 48.2 cm)
Sold 1.12.78 in London for £70,000 ($133,000)
From the collection of the late Baron Hatvany
Traditionally ascribed to Piero della Francesca, this picture was first attributed to Pesellino by Mrs Berenson

TOMMASO DI STEFANO LUNETTI:
The Adoration of the Shepherds
On panel
28½ × 19½ in. (72.3 × 49.5 cm)
Sold 29.6.79 in London for
£42,000 ($88,200)
From the collection of the Duke of
Wellington, MVO, OBE, MC
One of the large number of
pictures from the Spanish Royal
Collection found in the baggage train
of Joseph Bonaparte after the battle
of Vittoria in 1813 and subsequently
presented to the 1st Duke of
Wellington by King Ferdinand VII
of Spain

JUAN VAN DER HAMEN Y LEON: *Seedcakes on Dishes, a Bottle and a Glass Flask by a Box, with Walnuts, on a Ledge*
Signed and dated 1622
22½ × 37¾ in. (57 × 96 cm)
Sold 11.1.79 in New York for $140,000 (£73,684)
A hitherto unrecorded work by one of the leading Spanish still-life painters of the 17th century

GIULIO CESARE PROCACCINI:
*Madonna and Child with the
Infant Saint John the Baptist
and Attendant Angels*
On panel
19 ½ × 14 in.
(49.5 × 35.5 cm)
Sold 1.12.78 in London for
£150,000 ($285,000)
This was perhaps the first
picture by the artist to
reach England and was
owned by King Charles I
It was sold from his collection
in 1649 for £7 and later
fetched 25 guineas in the
sale of Thomas Turton,
Bishop of Ely, at Christie's
in 1864

GIOVANNI ANTONIO CANAL, IL CANALETTO: *View of Greenwich from the River with numerous Vessels*
23¼ × 37 in. (59.1 × 94 cm)
Sold 29.6.79 in London for £140,000 ($294,000)
From the collection of Major-General Sir George Burns, KCVO, CB, DSO, OBE, MC
This is one of three versions of the subject painted by Canaletto during his visit to England. It was sold in the Duke of Cambridge's sale in our rooms in 1904 for 220 guineas

FRANCESCO GUARDI:
*San Giorgio Maggiore,
Venice, seen from the
Giudecca*
18¼ × 15½ in.
(46.3 × 39.4 cm)
Sold 1.12.78 in
London for £75,000
($142,500)
Sold on behalf of the
Judith E. Wilson Fund
of the University of
Cambridge
A closely related
picture is in the
National Gallery of
Scotland

JEAN-FRANÇOIS DE TROY: *Time Unveiling Truth*
Signed and dated 1733
80 × 82 in. (203 × 208 cm)
Sold in London by private treaty
This major work by de Troy was owned by Laetitia Buonaparte, Madame Mère, and was later in the
Shrewsbury collection at Alton Towers, where it was sold by Christie's for 51 guineas in 1857

FRANCESCO ZUCCARELLI, RA: *Wooded Landscape*
24 × 37 in. (61 × 94 cm)
Sold 11.1.79 in New York for $49,500 (£26,052)

LUCAS CRANACH THE ELDER: *Judith with the Head of Holofernes*
Signed with the artist's device and dated 1525
On panel
5 ½ in. (14 cm) diameter
Sold 1.12.78 in London for £65,000 ($123,500)
From the collection of the late Baron Hatvany

HERRI MET DE BLES: *Saint Jerome in Penitence in a fantastic Landscape* and *The Temptation of Saint Anthony with a Burning Village Beyond*
In painted circles, on panel
5 × 5 in. (12.7 × 12.7 cm)
Sold 4.5.79 in London for £42,000 ($84,000)

JAN BRUEGHEL THE ELDER: *Wooded River Landscape with numerous Peasants and Travellers outside a Village*
Signed and dated 1616, on copper
10 × 14½ in. (25.3 × 36.8 cm)
Sold 29.6.79 in London for £400,000 (£840,000)
Sold by order of the Beneficiaries of the late Hans Mettler
Record auction price for a work by this artist
This picture is first recorded at Mannheim in 1731 in the collection of the Elector Karl Theodor of Bavaria
and was later at Munich

JAN BRUEGHEL THE ELDER and HENDRICK VAN BALEN: *Allegory of the Elements*
On panel
24 × 36½ in. (61 × 92.5 cm)
Sold 11.1.79 in New York for $85,500 (£44,736)

PIETER BRUEGHEL THE YOUNGER: *Extensive River Landscape with a Village Kermesse and Peasants dancing round a Maypole*
Indistinctly signed and dated 1626
Canvas transferred from panel
20 ½ × 30 in. (52 × 76 cm)
Sold 30.3.79 in London for £160,000 ($320,000)

ADRIAEN PIETERSZ. VAN DE VENNE: *Jeu de Paume in the Garden of a Palace*
Signed, on panel
6¼ × 8½ in. (15.8 × 21.6 cm)
Sold 30.3.79 in London for £65,000 ($130,000)
One of a pair of panels once in the collection of Ralph Bernal, in whose sale at Christie's in 1855 they fetched 41 guineas. They were subsequently sold here in 1889 (88 guineas), 1918 (480 guineas) and 1932 (95 guineas)

JOOS DE MOMPER THE YOUNGER: *Autumn: the Market Place at Lierre with numerous Figures and Shipping in a Dock*
One from a set of *The Four Seasons*
On panel
29 ½ × 41 ½ in. (75 × 105 cm)
Sold 30.3.79 in London for £80,000 ($160,000)

JOOS DE MOMPER THE YOUNGER: *Winter: an extensive Winter Landscape with a Village by a River, Figures on the Ice and numerous Peasants*
One from a set of *The Four Seasons*
On panel
29½ × 41½ in. (75 × 105 cm)
Sold 30.3.79 in London for £140,000 ($280,000)

SIR PETER PAUL RUBENS: *Saint Clara of Assisi displaying the Pyx on a Hilltop above the Camp of the Saracens*
Inscribed, on panel
11 × 14½ in. (28 × 36.3 cm)
Sold 1.12.78 in London for £60,000 ($114,000)
Purchased by the City of Antwerp
A *modello* executed in 1620 for one of the compartments of Rubens's ceiling decoration in the Jesuit Church at Antwerp which was destroyed by fire in 1718

DAVID TENIERS THE YOUNGER: *The Temptation of Saint Anthony*
Signed, on panel
16¾ × 21¾ in. (42.5 × 55.3 cm)
Sold 29.6.79 in London for £55,000 ($115,500)

JAN VAN GOYEN: *Wooded River Landscape*
Signed with initials and dated 1633, on panel
14½ × 25¼ in. (37 × 64 cm)
Sold 11.1.79 in New York for $85,000 (£44,736)

SALOMON JACOBSZ. VAN RUYSDAEL: *Beach at Egmond-aan-Zee with Figures, Carts and Boats*
Signed with initials and dated 1652, on panel
20¼ × 32 in. (51.4 × 81.3 cm)
Sold 29.6.79 in London for £60,000 ($126,000)

JAN VAN DE CAPPELLE: *Estuary in a Calm with Pinks, Kaags and a States Yacht at anchor*
Canvas transferred from panel
33¼ × 44¾ in. (85.5 × 113.5 cm)
Sold 29.6.79 in London for £510,000 ($1,071,000)
Sold by order of the Trustees of the late Lord Hillingdon
Record auction price for a work by this artist

WILLEM VAN DE VELDE THE YOUNGER: *Dutch Men-o'-War in a Light Breeze, a States Yacht saluting a Fleet of Dutch East-Indiamen*
Signed and dated 1654
19½ × 25½ in. (49.4 × 64.7 cm)
Sold 30.3.79 in London for £65,000 ($130,000)
From the collection of Major Leonard Dent, DSO
Previously sold at Christie's in 1873 (730 guineas) and 1886 (300 guineas)

CORNELIS DE VOS: *Portrait of
a Young Girl*
On panel
32 × 23¼ in.
(81 × 61.5 cm)
Sold 11.1.79 in New York
for $75,000 (£39,473)

GERARD DOU: *Old Woman seated by a Spinning Wheel, drinking Soup from an Earthenware Pot*
Signed, on panel
20 × 16 in.
(50.7 × 40.6 cm)
Sold 4.5.79 in London for £110,000 ($220,000)
From the collection of Dennis Lennox, Esq., removed from Downton Castle

BALTHASAR VAN DER AST: *Tulips, a Carnation, an Iris, and other Flowers in a Glass Vase, with Shells, a Lizard, and a Butterfly and Insects, on a Ledge*
Signed, on panel
21½ × 14 in. (55 × 36 cm)
Sold 11.1.79 in New York for
$255,000 (£134,210)

JAN VAN OS: *Mixed Flowers and Pineapples in an Urn on a Stone Plinth with other Fruit and Flowers, a Bird's Nest and a Cat*
Signed, on panel
34½ × 27½ in.
(87 × 69.9 cm)
Sold 29.6.79 in London for £70,000 ($147,000)

ROBERT GARDELLE: Two views of Geneva
From a set of four
Engraved by the artist
22¾ × 55¼ in. (57.8 × 140.2 cm)
Sold 29.6.79 in London for £35,000 ($73,500)
Sold on behalf of the Trustees of the Goodwood Collections

JACOB VAN RUISDAEL:
Norwegian Landscape,
with a Cascade
Signed
25 ½ × 21 in.
(65 × 53.5 cm)
Sold 11.1.79 in New
York for $90,000
(£47,368)

ISAAC FULLER: *King Charles II Asleep in the Lap of Colonel Carless in the Branches of the Boscobel Oak*
One of a set of five pictures depicting the escape of King Charles II after the Battle of Worcester
83 ¼ × 124 in. (211 × 314.8 cm)
Sold 23.3.79 in London for £35,000 ($70,000)
Sold on behalf of the Trustees of the 6th Earl of Arran's Will Trust
Purchased for the National Portrait Gallery

JOHN WOOTTON: *Huntsmen and Hounds in a Wooded Landscape*
40 × 49 in. (101.6 × 124.5 cm)
Sold 22.6.79 in London for £20,000 ($42,000)
Sold by order of the Executors of the late A. M. G. Kidston

CLIFTON TOMSON: *Mares and Foals in an extensive Wooded Landscape*
Signed and dated Nottingham 1811
51½ × 72½ in. (130.8 × 184 cm)
Sold 24.11.78 in London for £22,000 ($44,000)
Record auction price for a work by this artist
Probably the picture owned by Richard Watt of Bishop Burton and sold at his sale in our rooms in 1892 for 20 guineas

GEORGE STUBBS, ARA: *Dark Bay and a Grey in a Wooded Landscape*
Signed
23½ × 27½ in. (59.7 × 69.8 cm)
Sold 22.6.79 in London for £60,000 ($126,000)

SIR FRANCIS GRANT, PRA: *The Melton Hunt going to draw Ram's Head Cover*
35 × 60 in. (88.9 × 152.4 cm)
Sold 22.6.79 in London for £30,000 ($63,000)
From the collection of the Duke of Wellington, MVO, OBE, MC
Bought from the artist by the 1st Duke of Wellington in 1839 for 500 guineas

HENRY ALKEN, SEN:
The Meet and *Over the Fence*
Two from a set of four, all
signed
9¾ × 13¾ in.
(24.5 × 35 cm)
Sold 22.6.79 in London for
£35,000 ($73,500)

JOHN FRANCIS RIGAUD:
*Portrait of Joseph
Nollekens the Sculptor
with the Bust of Laurence
Sterne*
29½ × 24½ in.
(74.9 × 62.2 cm)
Sold 23.3.79 in
London for £9,000
($18,000)

SIR JOSHUA REYNOLDS, PRA: *Portrait of the Rt. Hon. John Hely Hutchinson*
48¾ × 39 in.
(123.8 × 99.1 cm)
Sold 22.6.79 in London for £26,000 ($54,600)
From the collection of Major-General Sir George Burns, KCVO, CB, DSO, OBE, MC
Purchased by the National Gallery of Ireland
The sitter is shown in his robes as Provost of Trinity College, Dublin

WILLIAM HODGES: *Point Venus from Matavai Bay, Tahiti*
11 × 15 in. (27.9 × 38.2 cm)
Sold 23.3.79 in London for £11,000 ($22,000)
From the collection of John Quilter, Esq.
William Hodges was the official artist on Cook's second voyage of discovery. Cook anchored twice in Matavai Bay, between 26 and 31 August 1773, and 22 April and 14 May 1774, and Hodges made several drawings from which oil paintings were subsequently developed; a variant of this picture is in the National Maritime Museum

ALEXANDER NASMYTH:
Portrait of John Cockburn
Ross, of Rochester and
Shadwick
35 × 27¼ in.
(88.8 × 69.2 cm)
Sold 23.3.79 in London
for £14,000 ($28,000)
From the collection of
the late Sir Richard
Jessel

EDWARD PRITCHETT: *View of the Piazzetta, the Doge's Palace, the Dogana and the Church of Santa Maria Della Salute, Venice, with a Procession*
44¾ × 63¾ in. (113.7 × 161.7 cm)
Sold 22.6.79 in London for £26,000 ($54,600)
From the collection of Major-General Sir George Burns, KCVO, CB, DSO, OBE, MC

FREDERICK RICHARD LEE, RA: *Waiting for the Ferry*
Signed and dated 1838
49 ¼ × 76 ½ in. (125.2 × 193.8 cm)
Sold 2.2.79 in London for £16,000 ($32,000)
Record auction price for a work by this artist
Previously sold at Christie's in 1873 (215 guineas), 1925 (19 guineas), 1928 (44 guineas) and 1950 (231 guineas)

J. F. Lewis

PHILIP HOOK

John Frederick Lewis's *An Intercepted Correspondence,* which made the world record price for a Victorian picture of £220,000 ($440,000), is a sumptuous work by the greatest of the English Orientalist painters. All the most popular and accomplished Lewis ingredients are here: glorious costume, intricate lattice-work, superb rendering of reflected colour, and a shimmering view of the rooftops of Cairo glimpsed beyond the harem interior.

Lewis had a close association with the East, and even lived in Cairo for ten years from 1841. He produced a series of pictures of harems (this one was painted in 1869) and evidently immersed himself in the Orient. Yet, despite his inside knowledge of the subject, he has also tailored the scene to meet the specifically European demands of the Royal Academy and its patrons. Having titillated his English public by the very nature of the exotic scenario of the harem, he goes even further by making it conform to the classic Victorian urge that a picture should tell a story. The title, *An Intercepted Correspondence,* suggests the drama that is unfolding: one of the Pasha's beautiful young ladies has been conducting a clandestine and forbidden romance; *billets doux* have been exchanged, and have fallen into the wrong hands; the incriminating evidence has been presented to the Pasha; and now the unfortunate (and somewhat petulant-looking) culprit is being brought in to stand judgement before him. It is an Eastern reworking of the Diana and Callisto theme, rendered suitable for the Victorian drawing-room.

The extraordinarily high price paid for the picture reflects various trends in the 19th-century market. One is the continuing interest in Orientalist subjects, particularly this sort of highly-finished, technically brilliant work. Another is the growing acclaim with which American public collections view the major examples of Victorian painting. And thirdly there is the general reappraisal of the last century which suggests that it will not be long before its best productions reach the Old Master league for prices, something hard to imagine even ten years ago.

JOHN FREDERICK LEWIS, RA: *An Intercepted Correspondence, Cairo*
Signed and dated 1869, on panel
30 × 35 in. (76.1 × 88.8 cm)
Sold 25.5.79 in London for £220,000 ($440,000)
Record auction price for a work by this artist
and for a Victorian picture

JAMES ARCHER, RSA: *Summertime, Gloucestershire*
29 ¼ × 41 in. (74.2 × 104.2 cm)
Sold 25.5.79 in London for £34,000 ($68,000)
From the collection of David Kelly, Esq.
Record auction price for a work by this artist

SIR EDWARD COLEY BURNE-JONES, BT, ARA: *Green Summer*
Signed with initials and dated 1868
25 ½ × 41 ¾ in. (64.7 × 106.1 cm)
Sold 25.5.79 in London for £48,000 ($96,000)
Record auction price for a work by this artist
Painted in 1868 and later sold to William Graham, MP, one of the artist's principal patrons, and sold at his sale in our rooms in 1886 for 500 guineas

EDWARD LEAR: *Mount Kinchinjunga, from Darjeeling*
Signed with monogram and dated 1877
73 × 113 in. (185.2 × 287 cm)
Sold 20.7.79 in London for £70,000 ($161,000)
From the collection of Mrs J. Webberley
Record auction price for a painting by this artist

JOHN AUSTEN FITZGERALD: *The Fairy's Funeral*
Signed, shaped top
9 ¾ × 11 ¾ in. (24.7 × 29.8 cm)
Sold 25.5.79 in London for £11,000 ($22,000)
Record auction price for a work by this artist

JOHN WILLIAM WATERHOUSE, RA:
The Orange Gatherers
45 ½ × 31 ½ in. (115.6 × 80 cm)
Sold 25.5.79 in London for
£18,000 ($36,000)
From the collection of
The Lord Faringdon
Record auction price for a work
by this artist

JAMES JACQUES TISSOT: *The Artist,
Mrs Kathleen Newton and her Niece
Lilian Hervey by a River*
Signed, on panel
11 ½ × 7 ¾ in. (29.2 × 19.6 cm)
Sold 25.5.79 in London for £10,000
($20,000)
Kathleen Newton began to live with
Tissot in 1876, the year she had her
only child by him, Cecil George
Newton

ATKINSON GRIMSHAW: *Liverpool from Wapping*
Signed
23 ¼ × 35 in. (59.1 × 88.9 cm)
Sold 13.10.78 in London for £22,000 ($41,800)

SIR JOHN EVERETT MILLAIS, BT, PRA:
Dropped from the Nest
Signed with monogram and dated
1883
40 × 27 in. (101.5 × 68.5 cm)
Sold 13.10.78 in London for
£35,000 ($66,500)
From the collection of
R. B. Mossman, Esq.
Record auction price for a work
by this artist
Sold at Christie's in 1893 for 1,200
guineas and in 1972 for £6,825

Artists in their Studios

RICHARD ORMOND, *National Portrait Gallery*

John Ballantyne's series of pictures of artists in their studios offers a fascinating glimpse into the lives, surroundings and working methods of successful Victorian painters. Brush in hand, they are engaged in the creative act, often with a well-known masterpiece in front of them. Around lie all the scattered impedimenta of the studio: easels, model stands, lay figures, clothes, casts, portfolios, objets d'art, pieces of furniture and of armour. The scenes are carefully stage-managed, the small and rather stiff figures posed in meticulously detailed interiors. The quality of the pictures is variable, but the best have an engaging vivacity of touch, and a genuine sense of atmosphere.

Accessories are employed not only for picturesque effect, but to amplify the character of the sitters. Sir Francis Grant, the fashionable portrait painter, is shown in a large sparse room, with portraits of his brother General Hope Grant, Sir George Wingfield Digby in the hunting field, and an unidentified lady. By contrast, W. P. Frith's studio is attractive and intimate, the artist himself engaged in painting Princess Alexandra into his well-known royal marriage group. Sir Edwin Landseer sculpts one of his Trafalgar Square lions in Baron Marochetti's studio, which he borrowed for the purpose. Daniel Maclise is perched on a platform in the House of Lords at work on his fresco of the *Death of Nelson* — this is the most inventive of Ballantyne's compositions. David Roberts, an unexpectedly dandyish figure in dressing gown and smoking cap, looks on tolerantly as a small boy, who has just exchanged his racquet and shuttlecock for a brush and palette, touches on his picture of a town square; the open door and distant vista suggest the child's breathless arrival.

The portrait of Roberts is in essence a genre scene, that is, it tells a story about the life and personality of the artist. It is also a documentary record of a distinguished man at work. As a result it has an appeal quite beyond its merit as a work of art. Perhaps inspired by E. M. Ward's earlier series of writers in their studies, Ballantyne was satisfying the insatiable curiosity of the Victorian public for insight into the lives of famous men, and the nature of their genius.

John Ballantyne was born at Kelso in Scotland in 1815, a member of a distinguished publishing and literary family. He studied art at the Trustees' Academy in Edinburgh and the Royal Academy schools in London, and from 1831 regularly exhibited portraits and subject pictures in both capitals. Never very successful, he later taught at the Trustees' Academy, and on his retirement in 1869 moved south to London to become curator of the life school at the Academy. He died at Melksham in Wiltshire in 1897.

Ballantyne began work on the series of artists' studios in the later part of 1862. By April 1864

JOHN BALLANTYNE, RSA: *Portrait of Sir Francis Grant, PRA*
Signed and dated 1866, and signed and inscribed on a label on the reverse
27 ¾ × 35 ½ in.
(70.5 × 90.2 cm)
Sold 2.2.79 in London for £15,000 ($30,000)
From the collection of Mrs Marianne Skioldebrand
Now in the National Portrait Gallery
One of Grant's portraits of his brother Sir James Grant is seen in the picture on the right

JOHN BALLANTYNE, RSA: *Portrait of William Powell Frith, RA*
Signed
29 ¾ × 24 ¾ in. (75.6 × 62.8 cm)
Sold 2.2.79 in London for £18,000 ($36,000)
From the collection of Mrs Marianne Skioldebrand
Record auction price for a work by this artist

when the *Art Journal* first mentioned the project, he had completed eight, and others are variously dated 1865, 1866 and 1867. Apart from the *Landseer,* relatively little documentation has come to light about the individual portraits. The introduction here came from Frith, to whom Landseer wrote in February 1864 agreeing to meet Ballantyne and talk over the project, although he suspected the motives as being speculative rather than coming from any desire to elevate art. Later there was an acrimonious correspondence between the two when Landseer accused Ballantyne of publishing his designs for the Lions in advance. This took place at the time of the exhibition at Henry Graves & Co. during the winter of 1865-6, which was briefly noted by the *Art Journal* in January 1866. Some of the portraits were sold at this time, a few more chromolithographed by Vincent Brooks, but the provenance of the majority remains obscure.

1. Sir A. W. Callcott's painting room. Exh. RSA 1864
2. Thomas Creswick. Exh. Graves 1865-6
3. Alfred Elmore. Exh. Graves 1865-6
4. Thomas Faed. Scottish National Portrait Gallery
5. Thomas Faed. Christie's 1979
6. Thomas Faed (painting in Highland cottage). Sotheby's Belgravia 1974. Exh. RSA 1866
7. W. P. Frith. Christie's 1979. Exh. Graves 1865-6
8. Sir Francis Grant (dated 1866). Christie's 1979, now National Portrait Gallery. Exh. RSA 1867
9. Sir George Harvey. Scottish National Portrait Gallery. Exh. Graves 1865-6
10. W. Holman Hunt. National Portrait Gallery. Exh. Graves 1865-6 and RSA 1867
11. Sir Edwin Landseer. National Portrait Gallery. Exh. Graves 1865-6. Chromolithograph by Brooks (NPG)
12. Daniel Maclise (dated 1865). Christie's 1979. Exh. Graves 1865-6 and RA 1866
13. Baron Carlo Marochetti. Chromolithograph by Brooks (NPG)
14. Sir J. E. Millais. Exh. Graves 1865-6. Chromolithograph by Brooks (NPG)
15. William Mulready. Mentioned *Art Journal* (1864) as in preparation
16. Erskine Nicol. Exh. Graves 1865-6
17. Sir Noel Paton (dated 1867). Scottish National Portrait Gallery. Exh. RSA 1867
18. John Phillip. Scottish National Portrait Gallery. Exh. RSA 1867. Chromolithograph by Brooks (NPG)
19. David Roberts. Christie's 1979. Exh. Graves 1865-6
20. Clarkson Stanfield. Christie's 1979. Exh. Graves 1865-6
21. E. M. Ward. Mentioned *Art Journal* (1864) as in preparation

JOHN BALLANTYNE, RSA: *Portrait of David Roberts, RA*
Signed, and signed and inscribed on a label on the reverse
28 × 36 in. (71.2 × 91.4 cm)
Sold 2.2.79 in London for £13,000 ($26,000)

JOHN BALLANTYNE, RSA: *Portrait of Daniel Maclise, RA*
Signed and dated 1865, and signed and inscribed on a label on the reverse
29¾ × 24¾ in. (75.6 × 62.8 cm)
Sold 2.2.79 in London for £13,000 ($26,000)

Both from the collection of Mrs Marianne Skioldebrand

CORNELIS SPRINGER: *Town Square*
Signed with monogram and dated 50 & 51, and incised with monogram on the reverse
On panel
16 ¾ × 22 in. (42.5 × 55.8 cm)
Sold 20.4.79 in London for £22,000 ($44,000)
From the collection of Mrs M. Bastable

BAREND CORNELIS KOEKKOEK: *Mountainous Wooded Landscape at Sunset*
Signed and dated 1851, and signed and authenticated on an old label on the reverse
On panel
18 ¾ × 22 ¾ in. (47.5 × 58 cm)
Sold 20.4.79 in London for £18,000 ($36,000)

HEINRICH BÜRKEL: *Boy with Farm Animals outside a Barn*
Signed, on panel
10 ¼ × 13 in. (26 × 33 cm)
Sold 20.4.79 in London for £13,000 ($26,000)

OTTO FRIEDRICH GEBLER: *Feeding Time*
Signed
20½ × 31 in. (52.1 × 78.7 cm)
Sold 2.5.79 in New York for $60,000 (£29,411)
Record auction price for a work by this artist

MAX LIEBERMANN: *Stille Arbeit: A Young Woman Knitting in an Interior*
Signed
27 × 18 in. (68.5 × 45.5 cm)
Sold 20.10.78 in London for £50,000 ($100,000)
Record auction price for a work by this artist

FRANZ RICHARD UNTERBERGER: *The Canal Tolentini, Venice*
Signed
43 × 39½ in. (109 × 100 cm)
Sold 20.10.78 in London for £14,000 ($28,000)

ALEXEI ALEXEIEWITSCH HARLAMOFF: *Young Flower Girls*
Signed and dated 1885
42¾ × 56¾ in. (108.6 × 144.1 cm)
Sold 16.2.79 in London for £25,000 ($50,000)
From the collection of A. K. Karmer, Esq.
Record auction price for a work by this artist

GIOVANNI BATTISTA TORRIGLIA: *Helping Mother*
Signed
28 ¼ × 43 ½ in. (71.7 × 110.5 cm)
Sold 19.10.78 in London for £16,000 ($32,000)

WILLIAM ADOLPHE BOUGUEREAU: *Cupid*
Signed and dated 1891
60 × 34 in. (152.4 × 86.4 cm)
Sold 2.5.79 in New York for $55,000 (£26,699)

EUGENE DE BLAAS:
Die Heimkehr
Signed and dated 1912
38 × 28 in. (96 × 71 cm)
Sold 14.10.78 in New York
for $36,000 (£18,273)
From the collection of
Mrs Van Buren

CORNELIUS KRIEGHOFF: *Portage aux Tritres, St. Maurice*
Signed
8¾ × 12½ in. (22.2 × 31.6 cm)
Sold 16.3.79 in London for £10,200 ($20,400)

GEORGE DE FOREST BRUSH:
The Artist Sketching his Family
Signed and dated 1892, on panel
19¾ × 23½ in. (50 × 60 cm)
Sold 23.5.79 in New York for
$70,000 (£29,166)

CHARLES BIRD KING: *Pair of*
Portraits: President John Quincy
Adams, President James Madison
(After Wood)
Signed and dated Washington
1826 and inscribed on the reverse,
on panel
Both 24 × 19½ in. (61 × 49.5 cm)
Sold 23.5.79 in New York for
$45,000 (£18,750)
Record auction price for a work by
this artist

SEVERIN ROESEN: *Still Life: The Abundance of Fruit*
c. 1860
Signed
36 × 50¼ in. (91.5 × 127.5 cm)
Sold 23.5.79 in New York for $50,000 (£20,833)

THEODOR KAUFMANN: *On to Liberty*
Signed and dated N.Y. 1867
36 × 56 in. (91.5 × 142.5 cm)
Sold 23.5.79 in New York for $40,000 (£16,666)
Kaufmann was one of the Europeans who fled the economic and revolutionary turmoil of Europe in 1848, settling in
America. After serving with the Union forces during the Civil War, he conceived a number of major canvases to
commemorate the recent conflict. In addition to paintings dealing with Abraham Lincoln's assassination and General
Sherman at his campfire, he produced *On to Liberty*, which was widely exhibited and commented on by contemporary
critics

A Portrait Drawing of his Son by Liotard

FRANCIS RUSSELL

Few portrait-painters of the 18th century were so widely fashionable as Liotard. He painted members of the royal houses of England and Austria and France and of the princely families of Württemberg and Orange: he portrayed many of the most fascinating individuals of his time, Voltaire and Rousseau, Algarotti and Garrick: and yet it seems as though a very special role was reserved for his portraits of such Genevois families as the Tronchins, and above all for those of himself and his family, his wife and children and more distant relations. For it is in his pictures of them that the universality of his art is most clearly stated.

Liotard's activity was defined by the tastes and limitations of his times. He was a meticulous observer of nature and the evidence of his own collection of pictures establishes that he responded to such observation in the work of earlier painters, to the genre pieces of the Dutch masters and the clarity of vision of Italian artists like Cima, whose *Sacra Conversazione* (now in the Pierpont Morgan Library) he sent to Christie's in 1774. The long series of Liotard's self-portraits shows with what curiosity he considered his own appearance. Mere vanity had little place in his character and he describes himself with the utmost objectivity, hale in youth and febrile in age. The portraits of his family are of equal candour. He draws his wife with affection but is too scrupulous to accentuate her charm with a beauty she evidently did not possess, but presents his niece, Mademoiselle Lavergne, for the clear-skinned seductress that she was. Such indeed was the success of the pastel of her reading which he painted at Lyons in 1746 that a series of replicas were to follow, sold with such titles as *La Liseuse:* one such was sold to an English patron, presumably during the artist's first visit to London, and was later thought to be a portrait of the bigamous Duchess of Kingston, an understandable tribute to the model's appeal.

Like his portrait of Mademoiselle Lavergne, Liotard's drawing of his son is at once a portrait and something rather more. Jean Etienne Liotard the younger was born in 1758 and sat to his father in 1770. He is seen at breakfast, cutting butter to spread on the piece of bread held in his left hand, heedless of the presence of the onlooker. The drawing was used for a portrait exhibited at Paris in 1771 and at the Royal Academy three years later and has a spontaneity that is not altogether matched in the surviving version of the picture, now in a Genevois collection. The sitter was aware of the special quality of the drawing, for in 1778 he wrote to his mother that he was 'bien fâché' with his father, who had refused to send it to decorate his room in Amsterdam. Liotard was often unwilling to part with his work but in this insistance his reluctance was doubly understandable, as the drawing is not only a memorable portrait but also the artist's delayed response to the genre pictures of Chardin. For it is a portrait with more than a merely personal message.

JEAN ETIENNE LIOTARD: *Jean Etienne Liotard, the Son of the Artist, at Breakfast*
Red, black and white chalk on blue paper, some of the outlines indented
$18\frac{3}{8} \times 22\frac{1}{2}$ in. (46.7 × 57.2 cm)
Sold 12.12.78 in London for £60,000 ($117,600)
This drawing remained in the possession of the artist's family until the 1930s

PIETRO DA CORTONA: *Study of the Head of an Angel*
Black chalk, 7 ½ × 6 ⅝ in. (19 × 16.8 cm)
Sold 28.3.79 in London for £7,000 ($14,000)
An unrecorded study for the head of the angel in Cortona's fresco *An Angel and Putti with Instruments of the Passion* of 1633 in the sacristy of the Chiesa Nuova in Rome

JACOB DE GHEYN II: *Study of Three Dragonflies*
Traces of black chalk, pen and brown ink
6 × 7⅜ in. (15.2 × 18.9 cm)
Sold 3.5.79 in London for £8,000 ($16,000)
This unpublished drawing dates from about 1600, when de Gheyn painted a watercolour which includes a similar
dragonfly, now in the Institut Néerlandais, Paris

JAN LIEVENS: *A Farmstead among Trees*
Signed with initials IL
Pen and brown ink on Japan paper
8 ¾ × 14 ½ in. (22.4 × 37 cm)
Sold 12.12.78 in London for £4,500
($8,820)
From the collection of the late
Monsieur Francois Dolez

HERMAN VAN SWANEVELT: *A River
Landscape with two Artists looking at
Figures on a Bank above*
Pen and brown ink, grey wash
6 ⅝ × 10 ⅞ in. (17 × 27.8 cm)
Sold 3.5.79 in London for £4,000
($8,000)

PIETER MOLYN: *Marauders attacking two Caravans on a Wooded Road*
Signed
Black chalk, grey wash
5¾ × 7⅝ in. (14.5 × 19.4 cm)
Sold 12.12.78 in London for £3,000 ($5,880)

WILLEM VAN DE VELDE II: *The English Yacht Portsmouth*
Pencil and grey wash
11⅛ × 19⅜ in. (28.3 × 49.2 cm)
Sold 3.5.79 in London for £2,800 ($5,600)
This drawing is connected with a picture by the artist's father at Greenwich and is datable about 1675

JEAN ANTOINE WATTEAU:
*Studies of a Man wearing a
Tricorn Hat and a Landscape*
Numbered 8
Red chalk
$4\frac{7}{8} \times 6\frac{1}{2}$ in.
(12.5 × 16.7 cm)
Sold 12.12.78 in London for
£10,000 ($19,600)

JEAN BAPTISTE PILLEMENT: *Evening with a Herdsman on a Footbridge*
One of a pair
Bodycolour on silk
$5\frac{1}{4} \times 12\frac{1}{2}$ in. (13.5 × 31.8 cm)
Sold 28.3.79 in London for £3,000 ($6,000)

JACQUES HENRI SABLET: *Antiquary showing an Antique Statue to three Travellers in Rome*
Signed and inscribed Roma 1788
Pen and black ink and bodycolour
11⅞ × 15⅝ in. (30.2 × 39.7 cm)
Sold 10.7.79 for £3,300 ($7,293)

FERNANDO BRAMBILA: *A Girl on a Donkey at a Ford*
Watercolour and bodycolour
13⅛ × 9¾ in. (33.4 × 24.7 cm)
Sold 28.3.79 for £950 ($1,900)
Sold on behalf of The Lyons Trust
From an album collected by the Whig hostess, Lady Holland

GABRIEL LORY, FILS: *Castello di Bardi, Parma*
Signed, watercolour
11⅛ × 16⅞ in. (28.4 × 42.8 cm)
Sold 24.10.78 for £2,000 ($4,000)
Painted for Marie Louise, Duchess of Parma and widow of the Emperor Napoleon

All sold in London

JOSEPH MALLORD WILLIAM TURNER, RA: *Kidwelly Castle, South Wales*
Watercolour
11 $\frac{5}{8}$ × 17 $\frac{1}{8}$ in. (29.5 × 43.5 cm)
Sold 28.11.78 in London for £9,000 ($17,820)
From the collection of Eric W. Phipps

JOSEPH MALLORD WILLIAM TURNER, RA: *Cologne from the River with Figures bathing from Boats in the foreground*
Signed twice
Watercolour
9½ × 13 in. (24.1 × 33 cm)
Sold 19.6.79 in London for £22,000 ($44,000)
From the collection of T. F. Blackwell, Esq., OBE

BENJAMIN WEST, PRA: *An Artist sketching beside a Lady on a Horse in Windsor Park*
Signed and dated 1789 Windsor
Pen and brown ink, brown wash
10¾ × 18 in. (27.2 × 45.7 cm)
Sold 19.6.79 in London for £5,200 ($10,400)

86
HUMPHREY REPTON: *The Pump Room, Bath: Qui capit, ille facit*
Signed, inscribed and dated 1784
Watercolour
17½ × 23½ in. (44.5 × 59.7 cm)
Sold 21.11.78 in London for £3,800 ($7,600)

JOHN RUSSELL, RA: *The Two Sons of Thomas Pitt, standing in a Landscape, holding a Cricket Bat and Ball*
Signed and dated 1804
Pastel, 29½ × 24½ in. (75 × 62.3 cm)
Sold 19.6.79 in London for £12,000 ($24,000)

An Album of Drawings by John Scarlett Davis

JAMES ROUNDELL

According to Samuel Redgrave's *Dictionary of Artists,* John Scarlett Davis 'became drunken and of demoralised habits — got into prison and died before the age of 30'. This colourful vision of the bohemian artist is far from the truth. Scarlett Davis lived an ordered and happily married life and died in 1845 at the age of 41. The 173 drawings in the previously unrecognized album sold on 20 March further testify to his diligence and skill as an artist.

By comparison with some of his better known and more prolific contemporaries in the generation after Bonington, such as Callow, Boys and Holland, Davis's work rarely appears on the market, and this album of drawings adds considerably to our knowledge of his art. Included is a small self-portrait showing a sober and intelligent young man of about 21. A number of rapid and skilful views of Florence, preliminary studies for the unpublished series of etchings *Views of Florence and other Parts of Italy,* reveal his highly developed sense of space and perspective. There are vivid sketches of Greenwich Pensioners, no doubt happy to sit for the eager young artist who thereby built up a corpus of character studies to introduce into his pictures. Indeed the album contains five studies for the watercolour *North Transept, Canterbury Cathedral* (Whitworth Art Gallery, University of Manchester), itself a study for the major oil painting belonging to Scarlett Davis's patron John Hinxman. Hinxman was responsible for commissioning a substantial part of Scarlett Davis's artistic output and when he died in 1846, owned no fewer than 489 pictures and drawings by the artist. These were sold in these rooms in 1846 and 1848, realizing a grand total of £581.8s.0d.

The drawings in this album should provide valuable help in identifying many works still to be located. It is therefore appropriate that with the aid of a grant from the National Art Collections Fund the album was bought by the Museum at Leominster, Scarlett Davis's birthplace.

JOHN SCARLETT DAVIS:
Self Portrait
Florence (two studies)
A Greenwich Pensioner

Four studies from an album of drawings. Pencil or pen and brown ink, portrait pencil and brown
wash, six with some watercolour additions, one in oil on paper, several on tinted paper, all laid in
the album the leaves of which are watermarked BE & S, 1828, red leather boards, gilt tooled
design, the front lettered A.K.S. One hundred and eighty in the album.
Sold 20.3.79 in London for £10,000 ($20,000)
Sold to the Leominster Museum, Hereford and Worcester, with grants from the National Art
Collections Fund and The Victoria and Albert Museum

JOHN VARLEY: *Conway Castle from across the Estuary*
Signed and dated 1808
Pencil and watercolour
8 ¼ × 18 ¼ in.
(21 × 46.3 cm)
Sold 19.6.79 in London for
£3,000 ($6,000)

PETER DE WINT: *Extensive Landscape with a Rider, a Bridge and distant Hills*
Watercolour
11 ¼ × 18 in.
(28.6 × 45.7 cm)
Sold 19.6.79 in London for
£13,000 ($26,000)
Record auction price for a
drawing by this artist

EDWARD LEAR: *Jerusalem from the Mount of Olives*
Signed, inscribed and dated 1858 and signed again with monogram and dated 1860
Watercolour
11¼ × 17⅝ in. (28.6 × 44.8 cm)
Sold 21.11.78 in London for £4,500 ($9,000)

JOHN WHITE ABBOTT: *On the Dart from Holne Chace, Devon*
Signed with initials, inscribed and dated July 16, 1800 on the reverse of the mount
Pen and grey ink and watercolour
6⅞ × 9½ in. (17.5 × 24.1 cm)
Sold 19.6.79 in London for £4,500 ($9,000)

FREDERICK NASH: *The Mansion House from Poultry looking down Cheapside towards St Mary-le-Bow, with the Lord Mayor's Coach in the foreground*
Watercolour
31 ¾ × 26 ⅜ in. (80.6 × 67 cm)
Sold 21.11.78 in London for £4,800 ($9,600)
Sold on behalf of the Trustees of the Swithland Settled Estates

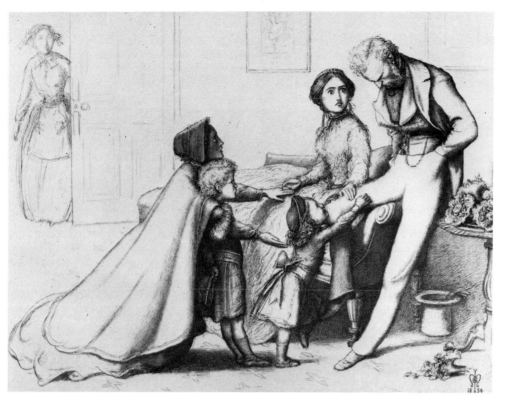

SIR JOHN EVERETT MILLAIS, BT, PRA:
Retribution
Signed with monogram and dated
1854
Pen and brown ink
7½ × 10⅛ in. (19.1 × 25.7 cm)
Sold 20.3.79 in London for £9,000
($18,000)
From the collection of E. G.
Millais, Esq., grandson of the
artist

ARTHUR RACKHAM: *Undine outside
the Window*
Signed and dated 09
Pen and black ink and watercolour
10¾ × 7⅞ in. (27.3 × 20 cm)
Sold 19.12.78 in London for
£2,800 ($5,320)
From the collection of the late
R. E. Sandell

CHARLES SAMUEL KEENE: *Two
Artists Painting by Lamplight in a
Studio*
Pen and brown ink
7⅛ × 4⅞ in. (18.1 × 12.3 cm)
Sold 19.6.79 in London for £2,800
($5,600)

ARCHIBALD THORBURN: *Partridges in the Snow*
Signed and dated 1892
Watercolour heightened with white on light blue paper
14 ½ × 19 ¾ in. (36.7 × 50.2 cm)
Sold 19.12.78 in London for £3,000 ($5,700)
From the collection of Mrs E. R. Whiteley

MYLES BIRKET FOSTER: *Skipping in the Road*
Signed with monogram
Watercolour heightened with white
11 ¼ × 15 ¾ in. (28.6 × 40 cm)
Sold 20.3.79 in London for £4,500 ($9,000)
From the collection of J. W. Blundell, Esq.

ALBRECHT DÜRER: *Knight, Death and the Devil*
Engraving, a very fine Meder A impression
Sold 24.4.79 in London for £15,000 ($30,000)
Sold on behalf of The Holker Estates Trust

ALBRECHT DÜRER: *The Apocalypse*
Woodcuts, the complete set of sixteen plates including title, in the
1511 edition with Latin text
Sold 27.6.79 in London for £16,000 ($34,560)

ALBRECHT DÜRER: *Saint Jerome in his Study*
Engraving, a fine Meder A impression
Sold 24.4.79 in London for £10,000 ($20,000)
Sold on behalf of The Holker Estates Trust

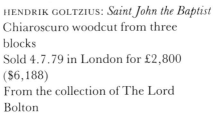

HENDRIK GOLTZIUS: *Saint John the Baptist*
Chiaroscuro woodcut from three
blocks
Sold 4.7.79 in London for £2,800
($6,188)
From the collection of The Lord
Bolton

GIORGIO GHISI: *The Philosopher, or the
Dream of Michelangelo,* after L. Penni
Engraving
Sold 24.4.79 in London for £7,500
($15,000)
Record auction price for a print by this
artist

REMBRANDT HARMENSZ. VAN RIJN: *Jacob
Haaringh (Young Haaringh)*
Etching, drypoint and burin, third
state (of five)
Sold 6.12.78 in London for £4,000
($7,760)

Rare Prints by Goya and Picasso

NOËL ANNESLEY

Dürer and Rembrandt, Goya and Picasso — these artists have long been recognized as the greatest print-makers, and yet it is a surprising fact that prints by all four are still readily available on the market, often in fine impressions. The season at Christie's has, moreover, been marked by the appearance of quite exceptional prints by the two Spaniards. This affords an opportunity to examine the common ground in their approach to this side of their art. While much of their preferred subject-matter overlaps, for example in an abhorrence of war and sympathy for the poor and oppressed, and in devotion to bullfighting, more notable is an eagerness to extend the frontiers of print-making as an expressive medium.

Goya's first series of etchings, the eleven sensitive copies after paintings by Velazquez in the Royal Palace, Madrid, were put on sale in 1778, when the artist was 32, and testify to the profound veneration he felt for the work of the 17th-century master. (Nearly two hundred years later, the equally admiring Picasso was to subject paintings by Velazquez, in particular *Las Meninas,* to endless, almost obsessive, variations in his own style.) Goya went on to develop the possibilities of etching and aquatint in his four long series of prints, beginning with *Los Caprichos,* a book of 80 plates published in 1799, but it was towards the end of his career that he became excited by the possibilities of the recently developed technique of lithography, which he first encountered at Cardano's Establecimiento Litográfica de Madrid in 1816 or a little later. His earliest known lithograph, *Old Woman Spinning,* is dated February 1819, when he was 73. In this, and in a few other prints of the time, he drew with pen and tusche (lithographic ink) on paper and then transferred the design by impressing the sheet on to the surface of the printing stone. Probably because he used too absorbent a paper, the resulting image was often imperfect, and he had recourse to strengthening it with black crayon. He may have become discouraged by imperfections in this technique, which would account for the gap between this and the next phase of his lithographic production.

Goya left Spain in 1823 following the restitution of Ferdinand VII and spent a few months in Paris, where he was struck afresh by the achievements in lithography of Carle and Horace Vernet and others. Later, when settled in Bordeaux with other Spanish exiles, he began to work directly on the lithographic stone, with the advice and help of the printer Gaulon. The extraordinary *Bull attacked by Dogs,* of which we sold an impression in April, setting an auction record for a Goya print, was probably the first fruit of this altered technique. While lacking the luminosity and richness of tone Goya was shortly to achieve in his celebrated *Bulls of Bordeaux* quartet, this fascinating print compared well with others of the eight impressions previously known, and was unusually well preserved, with wide margins. The composition derives from plate 25 of the *Tauromaquia* series of etchings with aquatint. Even rarer was the *Young Woman in*

PABLO PICASSO: *Tête de Femme, de Profil*
Drypoint, 1905, on Arches, a superb, extraordinarily rich impression printed with considerable dark grey tone, with much burr and ink in the deep plate edges, the lit areas of the face and neck delicately wiped to provide striking contrast with the overall tone, a working proof before the small number of impressions printed before the plate was steelfaced
Sold 5.7.79 in London for £48,000 ($107,520)

113

a Trance, only the fifth impression to come to light. By coincidence the fourth, now in the Museum of Fine Arts, Boston, also appeared for the first time at Christie's (*Christie's Review* 1970-71, *Goya's lithographs,* illus. p. 110). In the handful of lithographs he produced as an old man, Goya revolutionized the technique and opened the way for Delacroix, Manet and Redon, to name but a few of the exponents of lithography who succeeded him.

Picasso was still young when he embarked on his first series of prints in 1904. After extended visits from Barcelona to Paris in 1900 and 1901, he settled there in April 1904, and would have been influenced by the enthusiastic attitude towards print-making of the artists he then most admired, among them Toulouse-Lautrec and Steinlen. The set of fifteen etchings and drypoints known as the *Suite des Saltimbanques* treats a theme that engrossed him as painter and draughtsman during those years, the lives of entertainers such as acrobats, ballet-dancers and pierrots. These celebrated prints are most familiar in the paler impressions from the large edition of 279 published by Vollard in 1913 after the plates had been steelfaced. Occasionally, however, there appear impressions from the very small original edition, and the contrast in richness and power can be startling. One such was the magnificent *Le Repas Frugal,* Picasso's best-known print, dedicated to his friend Sebastian Junyent, which we sold three years ago (*Christie's Review* 1976, illus. p. 133). But perhaps even more remarkable was the small group auctioned this summer. Outstanding was the *Tête de Femme, de Profil,* richly inked and printed with a dark grey tone and with the highlights of the face and neck delicately wiped by the artist to brilliant effect. Similar subtlety and absorption in the technique of printing were evident in the other three plates. One of them, *Les Saltimbanques,* was an unknown first state before the addition of signature and date and other alterations, and it seems reasonable to suppose that all four were the artist's working proofs. The prices realized, far higher than those ordinarily attained for these subjects, reflected the fact that only in such vivid impressions is it possible fully to appreciate the beauty of Picasso's conception.

In the *Suite des Saltimbanques* Picasso established his mastery in the print medium in a fundamentally traditional manner showing the influence of his predecessors Rembrandt and Goya, before moving on in later years to pioneering techniques which mark him as the greatest modern print-maker.

FRANCISCO DE GOYA Y LUCIENTES: *A Bull attacked by Dogs*
Crayon lithograph with pen and tusche, a fine impression of this very rare print (only eight other impressions are known)
Sold 24.4.79 in London for £30,000 ($60,000)
Record auction price for a print by this artist

PABLO PICASSO: *Les Saltimbanques*
Drypoint, 1905, on Arches, a brilliant, rich impression, a working proof in an unrecorded first state before the addition of the artist's name and date in the lower right corner and other lesser alterations, printed with a delicate light grey tone and with much burr, the plate lightly squared in pencil
Sold 5.7.79 in London for £22,000 ($49,280)

GIOVANNI FRANCESCO COSTA: *Le Delizie del Fiume Brenta*
Etchings, title, publication notice and 72 plates from the series published in Venice 1750
Sold 4.7.79 in London for £12,000 ($26,520)

Veduta della Piazza del Mercato alle Gambarare
XXII

PIETER BRUEGHEL THE ELDER: *The Landscape with the Rabbit-Hunters*
Etching
Sold 24.4.79 in London for £17,000 ($34,000)
From the collection of Franz Koenigs

ANDERS LEONARD ZORN: *Mrs Gerda Hagborg II*
Etching, 1893, first state (of two), signed with
initial in pencil
Sold 5.7.79 in London for £1,300 ($2,522)
Now in the Zorn Museum, Sweden

PAUL GAUGUIN: *Nave Nave Fenua (Terre
Délicieuse)*
Woodcut printed in four colours, 1895, signed
in ink and dated 95
Sold 6.12.78 in London for £8,500 ($16,490)
From the collection of Mr Billy Hellsten

Above left:
JACQUES VILLON: *La Table Servie*
Drypoint, 1913, second (final) state
Sold 28.4.79 in New York for $14,000 (£6,862)

Above right:
JACQUES VILLON: *Le Potin*
Drypoint, aquatint and roulette printed in green, 1904, signed in pencil
Sold 16.11.78 in New York for $7,500 (£3,750)

GIORGIO MORANDI: *Natura Morta con il Lume bianco a sinistra*
Etching, 1928, second state (of three), signed in pencil
Sold 16.11.78 in New York for $7,500 (£3,750)

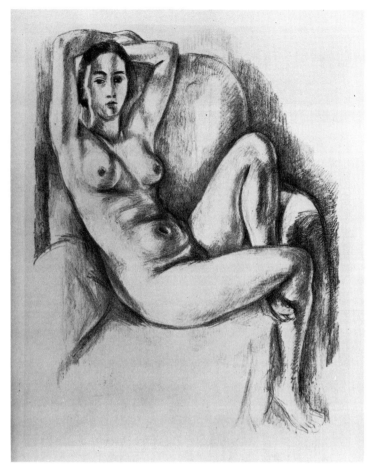

MAX BECKMANN: *Selbstbildnis mit steifem Hut*
Etching and drypoint, 1921, second state (of three)
Sold 28.4.79 in New York for $17,000 (£8,333)
Record auction price for a print by this artist

HENRI MATISSE: *Nu au Fauteuil, les Bras Levés*
Lithograph, 1924, signed in pencil
Sold 16.11.78 in New York for $24,000 (£12,000)

CHARLES MERYON: *Le Ministère de la Marine, Paris*
Etching and drypoint, 1865, a trial proof of the second state (of six)
Sold 28.4.79 in New York for $7,000 (£3,431)

EDVARD MUNCH: *Zum Walde*
Woodcut, with the two additional vertical blocks at each side, printed in four colours, 1897, signed in pencil
Sold 5.7.79 in London for £35,000 ($78,400)

EDVARD MUNCH: *Die Sünde, weibliche Aktfigur*
Lithograph printed in three colours, 1901,
signed in pencil
Sold 5.7.79 in London for £20,000 ($44,800)

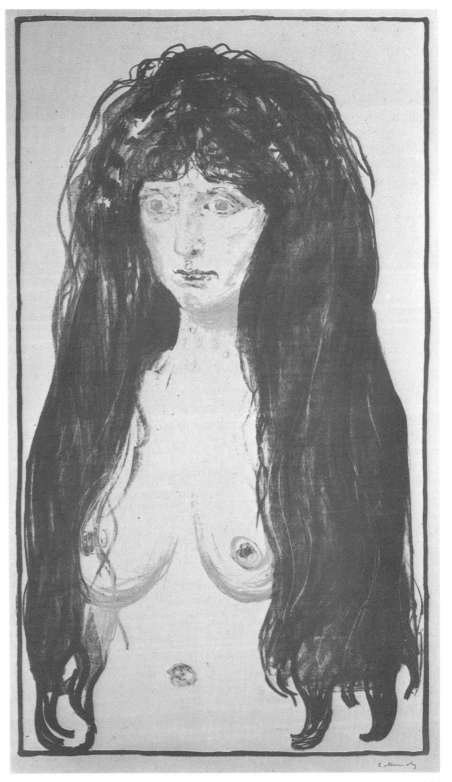

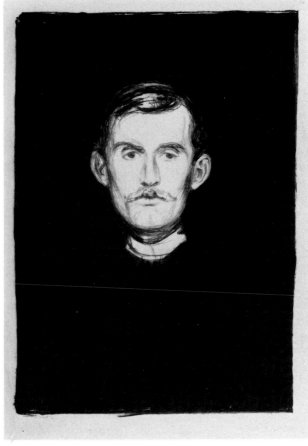

EDVARD MUNCH: *Madonna* (Eva Mudocci)
Lithograph, 1903, first state, signed in pencil
Sold 5.7.79 in London for £12,000 ($26,880)
Sold by order of the Executors of the late Miss Berta
Folkedal of Oslo

EDVARD MUNCH: *Selbstporträt*
Lithograph, 1895, second state, signed in pencil
Sold 6.12.78 in London for £8,500 ($16,490)
From the collection of Mr Christian Aall

EDVARD MUNCH: *Eifersucht*
Lithograph, 1896, signed in pencil
Sold 5.7.79 in London for £11,000 ($24,640)
Sold by order of the Executors of the late Miss Berta
Folkedal of Oslo

EDVARD MUNCH: *Madonna (Liebendes Weib)*
Lithograph, 1895, signed in pencil
Sold 28.4.79 in New York for $40,000 (£19,607)

MARY CASSATT: *The Bath*
Drypoint, soft-ground etching and aquatint printed in colours,
1891, eleventh (final) state, signed in pencil
Sold 28.9.78 in New York for $22,000 (£11,167)

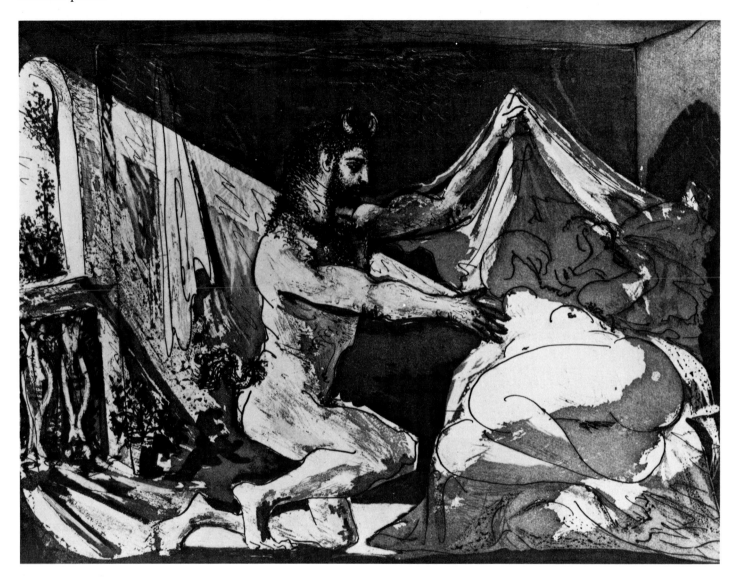

PABLO PICASSO: *La Suite Vollard*
Etchings and aquatints, 1930-7, the complete suite of 100, each signed in pencil
Sold 28.4.79 in New York for $230,000 (£112,745)
Record auction price for a single lot of prints sold in America

THOMAS HART BENTON:
Jesse James
Lithograph, 1936, signed
in pencil
Sold 23.3.79 in New York
for $3,800 (£1,900)

EDWARD HOPPER: *Evening Wind*
Etching, 1921, signed in pencil
Sold 28.4.79 in New York for $7,000 (£3,431)

GEORGE BELLOWS: *Preliminaries to the Big Bout*
Lithograph, 1916
Sold 28.4.79 in New York for $5,000 (£2,450)

SAMUEL PALMER: *The Bellman*
Etching, fifth state (of seven)
Sold 27.6.79 in London for
£2,200 ($4,752)

SIR WILLIAM NICHOLSON: *The Alphabet*
Woodcuts printed in
colours, finished by hand,
1898, the set of 26 plates,
signed in pen and black ink
on the original mounts
Sold 6.2.79 in London for
£6,500 ($13,000)

WILLIAM BLAKE: *Illustrations of the Book of Job*
Engravings, title and set of
21 plates, final states,
published by Blake and J.
Linnell, 1825
Sold 6.12.78 in London for
£4,000 ($7,760)
This copy is signed by John
Linnell, the publisher of the
set, on the label laid on the
front cover. The label is
inscribed 'Proof' and the
respective prices are given
'Prints £3.3' and 'Proofs
£6.6' (probably in Linnell's
hand)

126

SAMUEL DANIELL: *African Scenery and Animals*
Coloured aquatints, title vignettes for Parts I and II, description of plates and complete set of 30 plates, published by Daniell, Fitzroy Square, London, 1804-5
Sold 27.2.79 in London for £7,500 ($14,250)

After JOHANN DANIEL BAGER: *Blumen und Früchte,* by J. G. Laminit
One of a pair of mezzotints printed in colours, printed and published by Schweizer, Heilbron, Germany
Sold 27.2.79 in London for £8,500 ($16,150)
From the collection of the late Arthur van Zwanenberg

JOHN RAPHAEL SMITH: *What You Will*
Stipple engraving printed in colours, published by Smith, London, 1 Jan. 1791
Sold 27.2.79 in London for £1,100 ($2,090)

JEAN FRANÇOIS
MILLET: *Paysannes
au Repos*
c. 1850
Signed
17¾ × 14½ in.
(45 × 37 cm)
Sold 3.4.79 in London
for £175,000
($350,000)
A previously
unrecorded painting

EDOUARD MANET:
L'Italienne
1860
29 × 23 ¾ in.
(74 × 60 cm)
Sold 31.10.78 in New
York for $400,000
(£200,000)

HENRI FANTIN-LATOUR: *Nature Morte aux Roses et aux Fruits*
Signed and dated 78
15 ⅛ × 14 ½ in. (33.8 × 37 cm)
Sold 3.4.79 in London for £55,000 ($110,000)
Sold by order of the Executors of the late Mrs M. C. Wemyss Honeyman
Record auction price for a work by this artist

CLAUDE MONET: *Argenteuil, Fin d'Après-Midi*
1872
Signed
23 ¾ × 32 in. (60 × 81 cm)
Sold 15.5.79 in New York for $350,000 (£171,568)
Sold on behalf of the Estate of Lawrence Lever
Sold at Christie's in 1964 for £39,900 ($111,720)

PIERRE AUGUSTE
RENOIR: *Portrait de Jean
Renoir*
1899
Stamped with
signature
16 ⅛ × 12 ¾ in.
(41 × 32.5 cm)
Sold 3.7.79 in London
for £180,000
($394,200)

Opposite:
EDGAR DEGAS:
*Femme Nue, de Dos, se
Coiffant (Femme se
Peignant)*
c. 1885
Signed
Pastel on paper laid
down on board
27 ¾ × 23 in.
(70.5 × 58.5 cm)
Sold 31.10.78 in New
York for $380,000
(£190,000)

CLAUDE MONET: *La Tamise à Londres, Waterloo Bridge*
Signed and dated 1903
25 ¾ × 39 ½ in. (65.5 × 100.5 cm)
Sold 31.10.78 in New York for $260,000 (£130,000)

CAMILLE PISSARRO: *Le Pont de Charing Cross, Londres*
Signed and dated 1891
23½ × 28¾ in. (59.5 × 73 cm)
Sold 31.10.78 in New York for $190,000 (£95,000)
From the collection of Mrs Meta C. Schwarz

The Mettler Sale

JOHN LUMLEY

There were some extraordinary prices on 2 July: £370,000 ($810,300) for a Toulouse-Lautrec; £260,000 ($569,400) for a Redon pastel; and perhaps the most amazing of all, £295,000 ($646,050; over 1 million Swiss francs) for a Hodler landscape. Three days earlier a Jan Brueghel I, one of two Old Masters from the same collection, made £400,000 ($840,000).

Twenty-eight pictures had come to London for sale out of 31 which had decorated the walls of a comfortable but modest suburban house in Switzerland (the family kept an early Hodler landscape, a very small Redon flowerpiece and a Derain portrait). Previously few people had known of their existence. Only the Lautrec and a minor Matisse landscape had been shown in an exhibition outside Switzerland since the war. Even in Switzerland the surprise caused by the publication of the sale catalogue was considerable, nothing, for instance, having appeared in that celebration of the wealth of private Swiss holdings of modern art organized by François Daulte in Lausanne in 1964. The two Cézannes had never been shown in public at all. The Matisse *Coucous,* after having been one of the key paintings in Roger Fry's Second Post-Impressionist Exhibition in London in 1912, had subsequently been forgotten about. Even Pierre Matisse, the artist's son, who has spent his life in the art market, had never heard of it. The Redons were completely unrecorded; and so on.

The collector of these pictures was Hans Mettler (1876-1945), a textile merchant in St Gallen. It was in 1900 that he joined the family firm, which was founded in the 18th century and is still in business today, rising to junior partner in 1912 and then senior partner in 1930. His enthusiasm for painting, possibly kindled by his wife's cousin Mrs Hedy Hahnloser-Bühler, was shared by his own cousin Arnold, whose twin brother had a gallery in Paris for some eighteen months before his death in 1930 at the age of only 26. This loss, combined with the coming of the Depression and the increased responsibilities of being head of the family firm, caused Hans Mettler to stop collecting. Thereafter he neither bought nor sold, leaving the pictures to his family with a life interest to his widow when he died in 1945.

Although the figures sound derisory nowadays, Mettler paid high prices at the time. His first major purchase was the Hodler *Thunerseelandschaft,* which cost him Sw. fr. 15,000 in 1915. That was £587. His van Gogh *Allée des Alyscamps* cost Sw. fr. 35,000 (£1,103) in 1918, and in 1929 he spent Sw. fr. 41,000 (£1,625) on the tiny Cézanne *Baignade,* which was to prove to be his last purchase. Comparative values also make interesting study. The Matisse *Coucous,* for instance, bought in the same year as the van Gogh, cost only one-fifth as much (Sw. fr. 7,000; £319), with the small and to modern eyes far less interesting Matisse landscape of the port of Cherbourg surprisingly close behind (Sw. fr. 4,062; £190) a year later. Also in 1919 came the early Hodler *Der Leser,* which must have been expensive when Mettler acquired it at a public sale in Zürich

HENRI DE TOULOUSE-
LAUTREC: *La Grande Loge*
1897
Signed
Peinture à l'essence and
gouache on board
21 ¾ × 18 in.
(55.5 × 47.5 cm)
Sold 2.7.79 in London
for £370,000 ($810,300)
Record auction price for
a work by this artist

for Sw. fr. 11,000 (£514). Another interesting comparison is the seemingly high price of the Renoir *Roses* (Fr. fr. 30,000; £571) in 1920 compared with either the Toulouse-Lautrec (Fr. fr. 50,000; £916) bought in 1922,or more particularly with the Brueghel and the Redon pastel, which were each bought in 1923 for only Sw. fr. 7,000 (£319).

It is interesting to speculate what Hans Mettler himself would have thought of his sale 34 years after his death. While it is safe to assume that the prices themselves would have seemed grotesquely high, he might have been pleased by some of the comparative figures. He is said to have admired the Lautrec the most of all his pictures, so it is appropriate that this is still the most praised today. He would also have been delighted that his Hodler *Thunerseelandschaft,* which set him off on the road to collecting, made such an outstanding price. Finally it is easy to imagine that he would have smiled at the knowledge that it was neither art dealers nor museums that dominated his sale, but rather discerning *amateurs* who will continue to enjoy his pictures of their own private collections, just as he did for so many years in his.

PAUL CÉZANNE: *Une Baignade*
c. 1875-7
7 ½ × 10 ½ in. (19 × 26.4 cm)
Sold 2.7.79 in London for £120,000 ($262,800)

VINCENT VAN GOGH: *Le Zouave Assis*
Signed 'Vincent'
Pen and brown ink
19 ½ × 24 in. (49.5 × 61 cm)
Sold 16.5.79 in New York for $280,000 (£137,254)
Sold on behalf of Brown University, Providence, Rhode Island
Drawn in Arles in June 1888. In a letter to his brother Theo around 27 June 1888 (ed. Thames and Hudson, *The Complete Letters of Vincent van Gogh,* London, 1958, vol.II, p.590, no. 501), the artist writes 'Let's talk of something else — I have a model at last — a Zouave — a boy, with a small face, a bull neck, and the eye of a tiger . . .' Again around 30 June, in another letter to Theo (ed. Thames and Hudson, *op. cit.,* no. 502), van Gogh writes 'Anyway I shall send you a drawing of the Zouave today. In the end making studies of figures so as to experiment and to learn will be the shortest way for me to do something worth while'

PAUL CÉZANNE: *Un Clos*
c. 1890
24 ¼ × 20 ½ in.
(61.5 × 52 cm)
Sold 2.7.79 in London
for £145,000
($317,550)

EDVARD MUNCH: *Bathing Girls*
c. 1895
Signed
Pastel
$31\frac{5}{8} \times 33\frac{1}{2}$ in. (80.3 × 85 cm)
Sold 5.12.78 in London for £75,000 ($145,500)
From the collection of Mrs Gerd Brodersen

EDVARD MUNCH: *The Lady from the Sea*
Signed and dated 1896
39½ × 126 in. (100 × 320 cm)
Sold 3.7.79 in London for £155,000 ($339,450)
From the collection of Mrs Wenche Stang of Oslo

FERDINAND HODLER: *Thunersee von Leissigen aus*
c. 1905
Signed
35 ½ × 39 ¼ in. (90 × 100 cm)
Sold 2.7.79 in London for £295,000 ($646,050)
Record auction price for a work by this artist

LOVIS CORINTH: *Selbstporträt mit seiner Frau und Sektglas*
Signed and dated 1902
38 ¾ × 42 ¾ in. (98.5 × 108.5 cm)
Sold 3.7.79 in London for £56,000 ($122,640)
From the collection of Mr K. S. Rolfes of Cape Town
Record auction price for a work by this artist

Matisse and the Energy of Colour

LAWRENCE GOWING, *Slade Professor of the Arts, University College, London*

Sometimes a most various and complex artist, and Matisse was both, suddenly offers in a single picture the simple essence of what he has to give. We follow him to a crucial point in his development and there, as if meeting him at the crossroads, we can look back along the way he has come and forward into the future, and find the achievement and the potential both reflected in one exceptional canvas. That is how it is with Matisse's first painting of *Le Jeune Marin*.

In 1907, when Matisse went to Collioure for the third summer in succession, the impact and the shock of the style that he had developed there were receding into the past. The cultivation of random, capricious-seeming contrasts of colour as the rhapsodic medium of delight had lost the fierceness that had earned Matisse and his friends the nickname of *Les Fauves*. It had achieved its idyllic summing-up in the elysian composition *Le Bonheur de Vivre,* exhibited at the Indépendants the year before. The spirit was gentler and more reflective but the colour principle remained as energetic as ever. In *Le Jeune Marin* the deep hues that made manifest the presence of shape immediately precipitated the opposite colour in the vacant space beyond its contour. Cyclamen pink provoked turquoise, grass-green called up apricot. We can watch the energetic principle at work across the upright of the chair back that the sitter leans on. Ochre evokes a turquoise blue, like an extract distilled from the navy-blue jersey. Brick-red stimulates violet, and then as the reaction wears thin, a ripple of turquoise eddies back to outline the navy-blue jersey that it sprang from. The result is a continuous poetic iridescence, spreading across the canvas like a vital mode of being in which the subject has its existence. The subject in fact takes on a new breadth — the boy sprawls across the canvas far more roundly and naturally than the disembodied wraiths of colour that peopled the interiors of previous years.

The life is livelier; it has even the morose watchfulness of the waterfront. The vigorous, dry scumbling of specific local colour, navy-blue and emerald, models the body with a roundness that looks not backwards to Fauvism but forward in quite a new, robustly physical direction. Fauvism was a brush-stroke style, descended from the separate touch of Neo-Impressionism; now the wholeness and the continuity of a body is rediscovered. *Le Jeune Marin* is allowed his own heroic anatomy, swelling biceps and a herculean thorax; there is a reminiscence of the massive straddling poses of Renaissance tradition, and of the Belvedere torso that lay behind them.

The boy who came to pose at Collioure — without doubt in 1907, as the artist's daughter tells us, rather than the year before, as used to be thought — was in fact the witness if not the instance of two distinct developments in Matisse's art, each as potent for the future as the other. In front of this compelling model the fabric of separate touches on the model of pointillism was found inadequate. The meetings of colour, which generated their own pictorial light, required not the spots of impressionist illusion, but areas and a kind of image mapped out in provinces of colour, allied in a chromatic interplay with a breadth that was altogether new. The lesson was repeated, but not improved on, in a second version of *Le Jeune Marin,* in which the tension of discovery was relaxed in looping curves of flat colour. The value that has lately been set on the earlier picture demonstrates again how sensitive an aesthetic barometer the transactions of the saleroom can be. After *Le Jeune Marin* there was hardly a sign of the disturbing separateness of touch that Matisse called *vibrato*; the way was open to the broad colour-provinces of later years.

Yet there was something even more far-seeing in *Le Jeune Marin*. The model who lolled against both edges and touched the top of the picture filled the space in a new way. Matisse returned to such images at intervals all his life, by turns in sculpture and in painting, until their body-like unity recreated the wholeness of art.

HENRI MATISSE:
Le Jeune Marin I
1906
Signed
39 ¼ × 32 ¼ in.
(100 × 78.5 cm)
Sold 3.7.79 in London
for £720,000
($1,576,800)
From the collection of
Mrs Sigri Welhaven
of Oslo
Record auction price
for a 20th-century
picture

HENRI MATISSE: *Coucous
sur le Tapis Bleu et Rose*
Signed and dated 1911
32 × 29½ in.
(81 × 65.5 cm)
Sold 2.7.79 in London
for £190,000
($416,100)

ODILON REDON: *Fleurs
Exotiques dans une Potiche au
Guerrier Japonais*
c. 1905-8
Signed
Pastel
35 ½ × 28 ½ in.
(90 × 72.5 cm)
Sold 2.7.79 in London for
£260,000 ($569,400)
Record auction price for a
work by this artist

CONSTANTIN BRANCUSI: *Fish*
c. 1924-6
Polished bronze on metal disk
5 × 16 ½ × 1 ¼ in. (12.5 × 42 × 3 cm)
Sold 31.10.78 in New York for $400,000 (£200,000)

PIET MONDRIAN: *Large Composition with Red, Blue and Yellow*
Signed and dated '28
On panel
48 × 31 in. (122 × 79 cm)
Sold 31.10.78 in New York for $800,000 (£400,000)
Record auction price for a work by this artist

GIORGIO MORANDI: *Natura Morta*
1957
Signed
11 ⅞ × 15 ¾ in. (30 × 40 cm)
Sold 3.4.79 in London for £28,000 ($56,000)

ALBERTO GIACOMETTI: *Annette au Chariot*
Signed and dated 1950
28 ¾ × 19 ¾ in. (73 × 49 cm)
Sold 31.10.78 in New York for
$180,000 (£90,000)
Record auction price for a
work by this artist

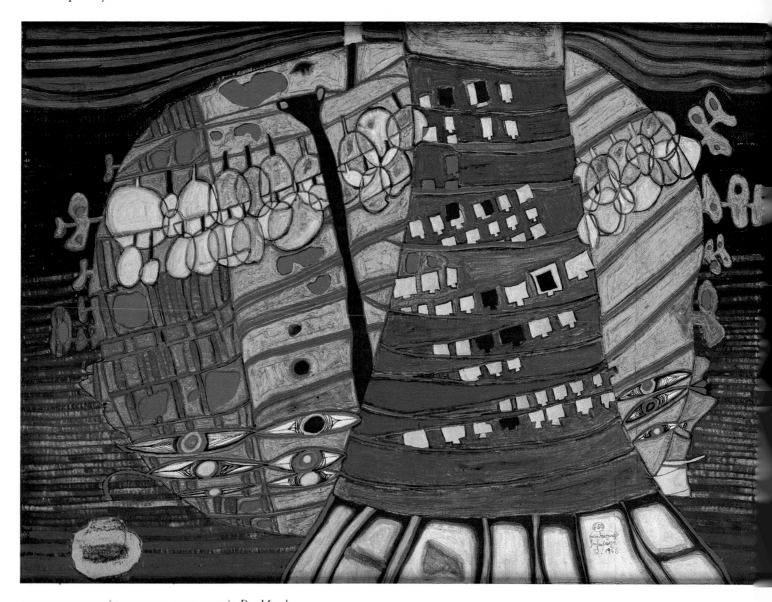

HUNDERTWASSER (FRIEDRICH STOWASSER): *Der Mond*
Inscribed, numbered 650 and dated 12.1966, signed and dated 1966 on the reverse
Mixed media on paper laid down on burlap
23 ¾ × 32 in. (60 × 81 cm)
Sold 3.7.79 in London for £15,000 ($32,850)

JEAN DUBUFFET: *L'Autobus*
Signed and dated '61, signed again, inscribed with title and dated again on the reverse
35 × 45¾ in. (89 × 116 cm)
Sold 15.5.79 in New York for $150,000 (£73,529)

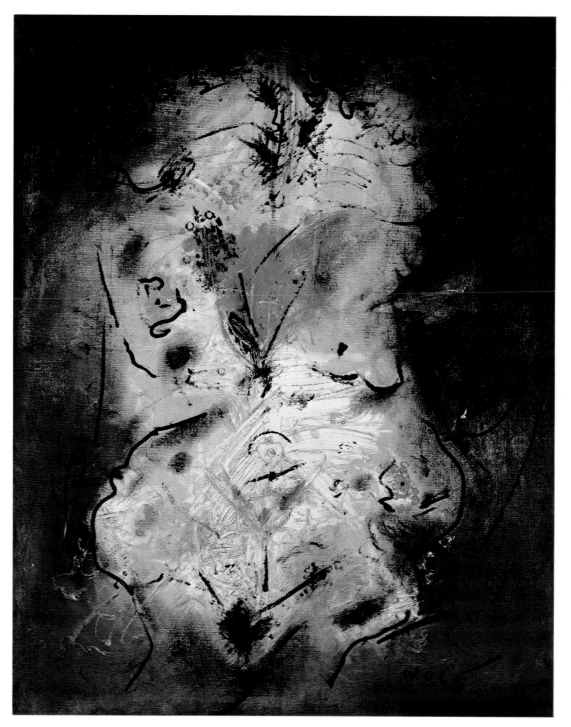

WOLS (WOLFGANG
SCHULZE): *Nu*
1949
Signed
Oil on canvas
32 × 25½ in. (81 × 65 cm)
Sold 3.7.79 in London for
£30,000 ($65,700)

ARSHILE GORKY: *Untitled*
1943
Oil on canvas
24 × 32 in. (61 × 81 cm)
Sold 18.5.79 in New York for $100,000 (£48,543)

JIM DINE: *The Studio (Landscape Painting)*
1963
All six panels signed (five with initials)
Oil and acrylic on canvas, wooden tray with glass and metal objects
60 × 108½ in. (152.5 × 275 cm)
Sold 3.11.78 in New York for $55,000 (£27,500)
From the collection of Mr and Mrs Eugene M. Schwartz
Record auction price for a work by this artist

EDWARD RUSCHA: *Noise, Pencil, Broken Pencil, Cheap Western*
1966, inscribed with title
Acrylic on canvas, 71 ¼ × 67 in. (181 × 170 cm)
Sold 18.5.79 in New York for $44,000 (£21,359)

ELLSWORTH KELLY: *Four Panels: Green, Red, Yellow, Blue*
Signed with initials on Panels A, B, and C on the reverse and dated '66 on the reverse of Panel A
Acrylic on canvas
Each: 52½ × 22½ in. (133 × 57 cm)
Overall: 52½ × 107 in. (133 × 271.5 cm)
The space between the panels measures 5 in. (12.5 cm)
Sold 18.5.79 in New York for $54,000 (£26,213)
Record auction price for a work by this artist

MORRIS LOUIS: *Aleph Series I*
1960
Bears Estate No. 190 on the reverse
Acrylic on canvas
105 1/8 × 141 7/8 in. (267 × 361 cm)
Sold 18.5.79 in New York for $170,000 (£82,524)
Record auction price for a work by this artist

FRANZ KLINE: *Painting # 3*
Signed and dated 1952 on the reverse
Oil on canvas
60 × 72 in. (152.5 × 183 cm)
Sold 18.5.79 in New York for $240,000 (£116,504)
Record auction price for a work by this artist

DAVID SMITH: *Jurassic Bird*
Signed and dated 1945
Steel
25½ × 35¼ × 7½ in. (65 × 89.5 × 19 cm)
Sold 3.11.78 in New York for $75,000 (£37,500)
From the Makler Family Collections

PHILIP WILSON STEER, OM: *Children playing in a Park, Ludlow*
1909
Signed
22¾ × 36 in. (57.8 × 91.4 cm)
Sold 8.6.79 in London for £7,500 ($15,450)
From the collection of
T. F. Blackwell, Esq., OBE

JAMES BOLIVAR MANSON: *Rye from across Fields*
Signed and dated 1913, dated Rye Aug. 1913 on the stretcher
21 × 25¾ in. (53.4 × 65.4 cm)
Sold 8.6.79 in London for £3,000 ($6,018)
From the collection of
T. F. Blackwell, Esq., OBE
Record auction price for a work by this artist

CHARLES GINNER, RA: *The Fruit Stall*
1914, signed
25 ¾ × 20 in. (65.4 × 50.8 cm)
Sold 17.11.78 in London for £9,500 ($19,000)
From the collection of Anton Lock, Esq.

WALTER RICHARD
SICKERT, ARA: *Easter
Monday, Helen Dumont*
c. 1908
Signed
20½ × 16½ in.
(52 × 42 cm)
Sold 2.3.79 in London
for £21,000 ($42,000)
Sold by order of the
Executors of the late
Mrs M. C. Wemyss
Honeyman
Record auction price
for a work by this artist

ROBERT BEVAN: *The Weigh House, Cumberland Market*
c. 1914
20 × 24 in. (50.8 × 61 cm)
Sold 8.6.79 in London for £17,000 ($35,000)
Record auction price for a work by this artist

AUGUSTUS JOHN, OM, RA: *David at a Table*
Signed
20 × 26 in. (50.8 × 66 cm)
Sold 17.11.78 in London for £10,000 ($20,000)
Record auction price for a work by this artist
David John (6 January 1902-1974) was Augustus and Ida John's first child and was for many years an oboist in the Sadlers Wells orchestra. He also worked as a postman and furniture remover

JOHN SINGER SARGENT,
RA: *Jerusalem*
1906
28 × 22 in.
(71.2 × 57 cm)
Sold 17.11.78 in
London for £12,000
($24,000)

EDWARD SEAGO: *Corner of a Norfolk Village*
Signed, on board
13¼ × 17¼ in. (33.6 × 43.8 cm)
Sold 8.6.79 in London for £6,500 ($13,390)
From the collection of Mrs L. M. Harrison

SIR ALFRED MUNNINGS, PRA: *The White Canoe*
Painted in 1924
Signed
20 × 24 in. (50.8 × 61 cm)
Sold 17.11.78 in London for £8,000
($16,000)

MONTAGUE DAWSON: *Far Away; 'The Black Adder'*
Signed
24 × 36 in. (61 × 91.4 cm)
Sold 8.6.79 in London for £17,000 ($35,020)
From the collection of J. G. Laird, Esq.
Record auction price for a work by this artist

SIR GEORGE CLAUSEN, RA: *Binding Sheaves*
Signed and dated 1905, inscribed with title on the stretcher
20 × 24 in. (51 × 61 cm)
Sold 2.3.79 in London for £7,500 ($15,000)

SIR JACOB EPSTEIN: *Dr Chaim Weizmann*
1933
Signed, bronze
18½ in. (47 cm) high
Sold 2.3.79 in London for £8,000 ($16,000)
Record auction price for a work by this artist

WILLIAM McTAGGART, RSA: *Harvest near Cowden*
Signed and dated 1893
24 × 36½ in. (61 × 92.5 cm)
Sold 4.6.79 in Glasgow for £11,000 ($22,440)
Record auction price for a painting by this artist

In 1978 Christie's made a further step in its expansion and took over the old-established Glasgow firm of auctioneers, Edmiston's. The newly decorated saleroom Christie's & Edmiston's opened on 4 June this year with a remarkable sale of 19th- and 20th-century Scottish paintings from the collection of the late R. Wemyss Honeyman, a Kirkcaldy textile manufacturer who had a considerable enthusiasm for the Scottish Colourists, especially Peploe. The sale marked a new level of prices for 20th-century Scottish painting, with bidding from both dealers and private collectors north and south of the Border. Outstanding prices included £13,500 ($27,540) for a *Still Life* by Peploe and £11,000 ($22,440) for a McTaggart. There were over fifteen records achieved. Although it was appropriate to launch the new venture with such an outstanding Scottish collection, Christie's & Edmiston's daily business will concern more general sales of pictures, furniture and objects and give a quick and expert service backed where necessary by specialist departments in London.

Although S. J. Peploe (1871-1935) was particularly well represented in the sale of the Wemyss Honeyman Collection (with no less than 23 pictures included in the catalogue), there were also fine works by the three other Scottish Colourists, Leslie Hunter (1877-1931), Francis Campbell Boileau Cadell (1883-1937) and John Duncan Fergusson (1874-1961).

All four painters owed much to the earlier Scottish group of artists who formed the Glasgow School, whose outright rejection of academic values paved the way for a return to the more vigorous handling of paint and expressive use of colour. With the example and inspiration given them by the Glasgow School, the Colourists were able to go still further. Foreign travel and the contact this gave them with the more advanced painting on the Continent was also a decisive factor in their development but, in particular, their frequent visits to the Côte d'Azur revealed a new and dazzling quality of light and brought them more directly under the influence of both Matisse and Cézanne.

No-one would pretend that the work of the Scottish Colourists equals the originality of their French contemporaries. Nevertheless, the best examples of these four painters, as shown in the Honeyman Collection, display great strength in their imaginative handling of the paint itself and their bold use of colour. Their vitality breathed a new spirit into the tradition of Scottish painting, whose subsequent development owes much to their vision.

SAMUEL JOHN PEPLOE, RSA: *Still Life of Pink Roses in a White Vase, with Book and Fruit*
30 × 25 in. (76.5 × 63.5 cm)
Sold 4.6.79 in Glasgow for £13,500 ($27,540)
Record auction price for a painting by this artist

175

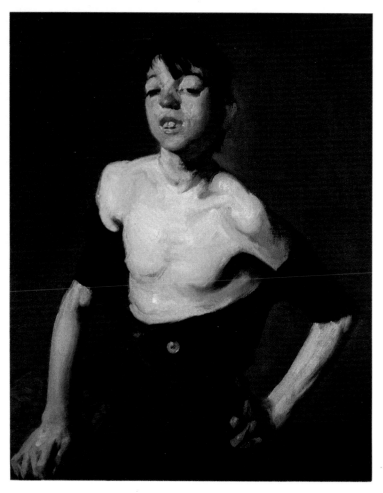

GEORGE BELLOWS: *Paddy Flannigan*
Signed
30¼ × 25¼ in. (77 × 64 cm)
Sold 23.5.79 in New York for $110,000 (£45,833)

NORMAN ROCKWELL: *Self Portrait*
33 × 27 in. (84 × 68.5 cm)
Sold 8.12.78 in New York for $42,000 (£21,538)
Record auction price for a work by this artist

BOOKS, MANUSCRIPTS AND AUTOGRAPH LETTERS

The Houghton Sale

GORDON N. RAY, *President, John Simon Guggenheim Memorial Foundation*

It was clear from the first that the sale of Arthur Houghton's library would take its place among the salient book auctions of history. The second quarter of this century saw at least the beginning of a number of other great American collections, for example those of C. Waller Barrett, Raphael Esmerian, Philip Hofer, Donald and Mary Hyde, Josiah F. Lilly, H. Bradley Martin, Lessing Rosenwald, John and William Scheide, Thomas Streeter, and Robert H. Taylor. Two of these have already been sold; others have become, or are clearly destined to become, parts of institutional libraries. Thus the Houghton sale represented almost the last chance for collectors to participate significantly in what has come to seem a legendary age of plenty.

Of course, Mr Houghton's standing as a collector is not to be assessed solely, or even principally, by the material offered in this auction. Missing were his Gutenberg Bible, his great Persian manuscript, his drawings by Fragonard for Ariosto, his Arnold Toynbee papers, and his remarkable collections of Lewis Carroll and Keats — not to mention many other treasures. (For a detailed account of his collection, see William H. Bond, 'Arthur Amory Houghton Jr.', *Book Collector*, spring 1957, pp. 3-15.) Some of these had been sold, some had been placed in institutions (notably the Houghton Library at Harvard and the Pierpont Morgan Library), and others are being held for future disposition. What remained was nonetheless the backbone of a superb assemblage of English literature, put together when books and manuscripts of first quality were for the last time freely available on the market. Certainly there had been no comparable sale in this field since the Second World War.

Interest in the event was further enhanced by the fact that it came as a surprise. It had been assumed that what remained of Mr Houghton's collection would go to the institutions which had already benefited from his munificence. Family considerations played their part in his decision, but there was also the fact that what remained on his shelves was for the most part a collection of high spots, more interesting to his fellow collectors than to researchers. So it came about that the special circumstances which go into the creation of an exciting occasion were abundantly present.

The most recent auction of comparable importance was that of Raphael Esmerian's collection of French illustrated books and fine bindings in Paris between 1972 and 1974. This sale had confirmed the status of 'beaux livres' on the international market, placing them on a par with books related to the history of science, medicine, and thought generally, which had for some time previously been the most active area of collecting. The impression had gained ground that in comparison English literature, for decades the preferred speciality of many British and American collectors, had lost much of its appeal. Certainly prices in this area had

WILLIAM BLAKE: *Songs of Innocence and Experience*
1789-(94?)
First edition and one of only three copies of the
earliest issue known, with the final plate 'A
Divine Image'
Sold 13.6.79 in London for £70,000 ($146,300)
From the collection of Arthur A. Houghton, Jr
Record auction price for a work by this author
and printer

hardly kept pace with those in the others mentioned. The aura of doubt thus generated had its effect on Christie's pre-sale estimates, based as they were on successive appraisals by two expert but conservative American dealers earlier in the 1970s. At any rate the low estimates totalled £651,520 ($1,361,677), the high estimates £880,250 ($1,839,722). These moderate figures provided a further incentive for active and enthusiastic bidding.

The first of two announced sales (comprising the letters A to L) took place in Christie's Great Rooms on 13 and 14 June under the alert and genial direction of J. A. Floyd. The audience was a distinguished one and it was treated to a stirring show. The proceedings throughout were dominated by four dealers, with John Fleming leading the way. This was appropriate enough, since Dr Rosenbach (whom Mr Fleming succeeded) had regarded Mr Houghton as 'the ace' in his 'royal flush' of customers (Edwin Wolf II and John Fleming, *Rosenbach: A Biography,* Cleveland and New York, 1962, p. 437). Mr Fleming's successful bids amounted to £374,290 ($782,266) (24.6% of the total realized). He was followed by Warren Howell, £287,400 ($600,666) (18.9%); Messrs Quaritch, £249,370 ($521,183) (16.4%); and Hans Kraus, £202,800 ($423,852) (13.6%). In all, the sale made £1,518,750 ($3,173,811), more than doubling the estimates, if one takes as a base the midpoint between low and high figures.

Mr Houghton attended the two sessions with members of his family. It is to be hoped that he was gratified by the results. Both his taste as a collector and his shrewdness as a buyer had been amply validated. A characteristic anecdote may be offered in illustration of these qualities, though it does not concern an item from this sale. In 1951, when the Rosenbach Company was in difficulties with what would now be called 'cash flow', Philip Rosenbach, who was temporarily in charge, directed Mr Fleming to sell the manuscript libretto of *Die Meistersinger* for $12,500, even though it had figured for years in the Company's catalogues at $55,000.

'That afternoon', it is related in *Rosenbach* (p. 582), 'Fleming walked around to Arthur Houghton's office and laid the manuscript before him. Houghton's poker face did not change when the price was mentioned; he merely remarked, "Have you any more at these prices?"'

Before proceeding to the main body of the sale, I should mention two groups of manuscripts quite outside the province of English literature. The first included a volume of charts and sailing directions used by pilots to navigate the Pacific coast of America in the mid-17th century (£65,000, $135,850) and a coloured maritime atlas of 1692, also Spanish, of the same part of the world (£65,000, $135,850). The second consisted of late 17th-century Pacific atlases and journals of voyages translated or edited by William Hack (five items; £288,000, $607,920). These rare and beautiful manuscripts, which accounted for about one-fifth of the total realized by the sale, were hotly disputed by Messrs Howell and Kraus, with honours even after the contest.

Spectacular prices, however, are now routine for this kind of material. The real test presented by the Houghton collection had to do with English literature. At least over the last twenty years less familiar fields, in which scholarly exploration was constantly leading to discoveries, had diverted interest from this venerable favourite, whose standard books for many collectors had come to seem commonplace, repetitive, and consequently boring. Would Mr Houghton's astonishing accumulation of authentic rarities, often in magnificent condition, rescue the field from its relatively depressed state? The answer was a resounding 'yes'.

Of course, different periods had different fortunes. There was only one early book of

The Book of Common Prayer
First issue of the first edition, the seventh
daye of Marche, 1549
Sold 13.6.79 in London for £50,000
($104,500)
From the collection of Arthur A.
Houghton, Jr

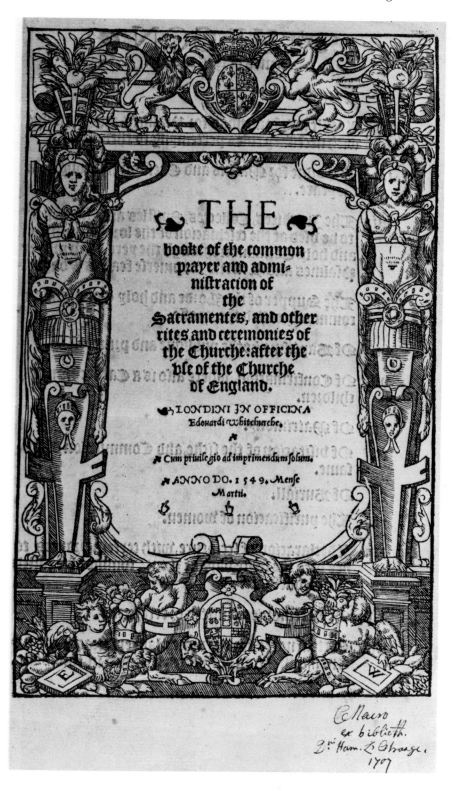

importance, Caxton's *Chronicles of England,* which brought a comfortable £62,000 ($129,580). The heart of the sale lay in the 16th and 17th centuries. Here a 'last chance' attitude prevailed among bidders, and with some reason. For such superb copies as Ford's *Broken Heart* (£2,400, $5,016), the three volumes of Gascoigne's poems (£24,000, $50,160; £14,000, $29,260; £15,000, $31,350), Herrick's *Hesperides* (£11,000, $22,990), King James the First's *Essays of a Prentise in the Divine Art of Poesie* (£13,000, $27,170) and Lovelace's *Lucasta* (£7,500, $15,675), even the sums noted were not excessive. Indeed, the principal manuscript of the period, a notebook of John Locke containing the earliest known draft of his *Essay concerning Humane Understanding,* seemed almost a bargain at £75,000 ($156,750).

The 18th century proved a comparative disappointment. In a sale where the manuscript of *Geist's Grave,* an elegy for a beloved dog which would hardly rank among the first 25 of Matthew Arnold's poems, brought £1,900 ($3,971), it was incongruous to find the manuscript of Thomas Gray's *Ode on the Death of a Favourite Cat,* an acknowledged masterpiece of English poetry, changing hands at only £4,200 ($8,778). As to the runs of books by Defoe and Gay, the condition of which often left a good deal to be desired, even the atmosphere of a great sale could not stir much competition. It was left to a fine copy of Blake's *Songs of Innocence and Experience* (£70,000, $146,300) to save the period's credit.

The true significance of the prices paid for Mr Houghton's 19th-century books and manuscripts will be best appreciated by those long familiar with the field. Though still not of comparable magnitude for the most part with those for works of earlier centuries, they in fact represented a quantum jump for the period. That Arnold's *Alaric of Rome* would bring £3,400 ($7,106), or one of a series of his notebooks £4,200 ($8,778), would hardly have seemed possible before the sale. Prices of £5,500 ($11,495) and £11,000 ($22,990) were not unexpected for two of Charlotte Bronte's microscopic manuscripts, but £3,500 ($7,315) for the volume of *Poems* which she wrote with her sisters was a surprise. Some 119 of Elizabeth Barrett Browning's letters to her family, documents of crucial biographical significance, were not expensive at £32,000 ($66,880), nor was a manuscript of her *Sonnets from the Portuguese* at £35,000 ($73,500), but it was impressive to find demand remaining strong for 23 other lots of letters and manuscripts by the Brownings, some of decidedly marginal merit. The bidding continued at the same level throughout the sale.

The auction was held in London at the wish of Mr Houghton, who has always entertained a strong affection for England. American buyers were reassured by the statement that 'since this collection has been consigned from outside the United Kingdom, there will be no difficulty in obtaining an Export Licence for any lot'. Probably the location of the sale made little difference, for ten perfectly mobile dealers paid 93% of the total realized. As to the ultimate destination of the books and manuscripts purchased, there was general agreement that most of them are returning to the United States.

The Houghton Sale may well give the same impetus to the market for exceptional books and manuscripts of English literature as the Esmerian sale did to the market for exceptional French illustrated books and bindings. The demonstration it provided that for really fine material there is an eager and widespread demand should help to bring this long-cherished speciality out of the doldrums. When the second half of the collection (M to Z) is offered at Christie's next June, a sale even stronger in books than the first, though perhaps not so rich in manuscripts, this prediction will be put to the proof.

ELIZABETH BARRETT BROWNING:
Sonnets from the Portuguese
Autograph manuscript
prepared for the first printed
version (1849-50)
Sold 13.6.79 in London for
£35,000 ($73,500)
From the collection of Arthur
A. Houghton, Jr

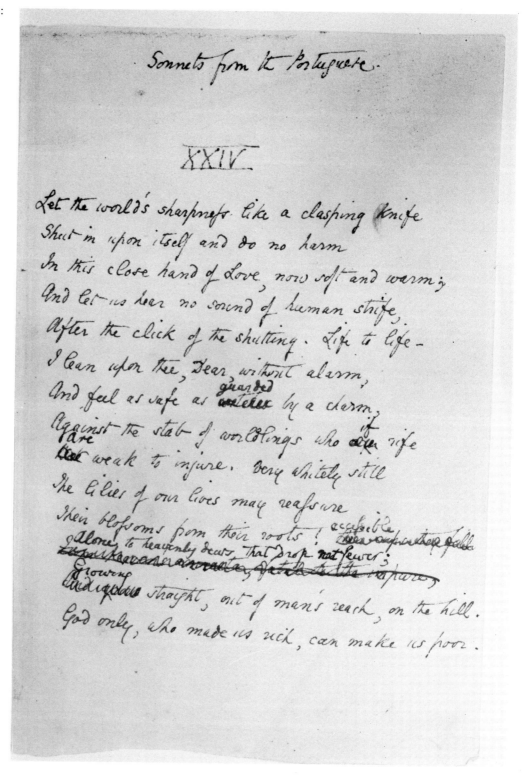

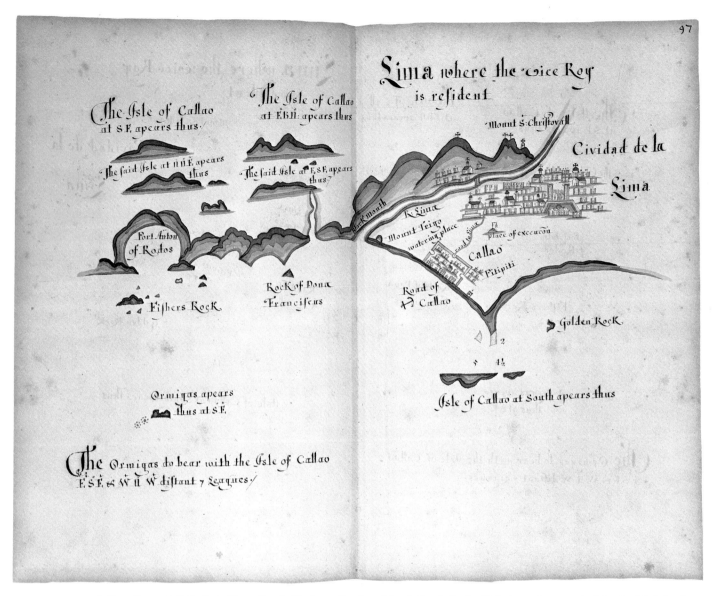

97

WILLIAM HACK: *A Descripcon of all the Ports Bayes Roads Harbours Bearings Islands Sands Rocks & Daingers between the Mouth of Calafornia & the Straights of Lemaire in the South Seas of America . . . carefully taken from the original Spanish Manuscripts & our late English Discoverers*
Manuscript maritime atlas, *c.* 1695-8
Sold 14.6.79 in London for £120,000 ($250,800)
From the collection of Arthur A. Houghton, Jr

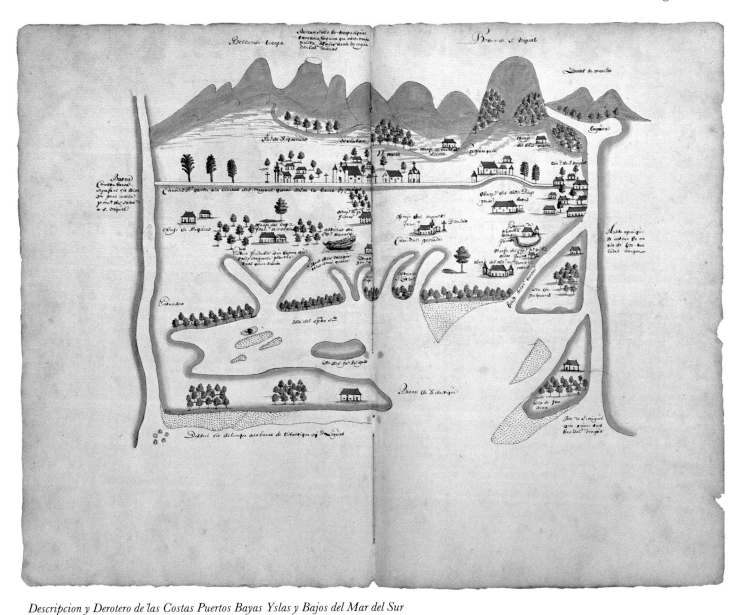

Descripcion y Derotero de las Costas Puertos Bayas Yslas y Bajos del Mar del Sur
(Description and Rutter of the Coasts, Ports, Bays, Islands and Banks of the South Sea)
Manuscript of 193 leaves describing the Pacific coastline of Central and South America, dated Panama 1692
Sold 14.6.79 in London for £65,000 ($135,850)
From the collection of Arthur A. Houghton, Jr

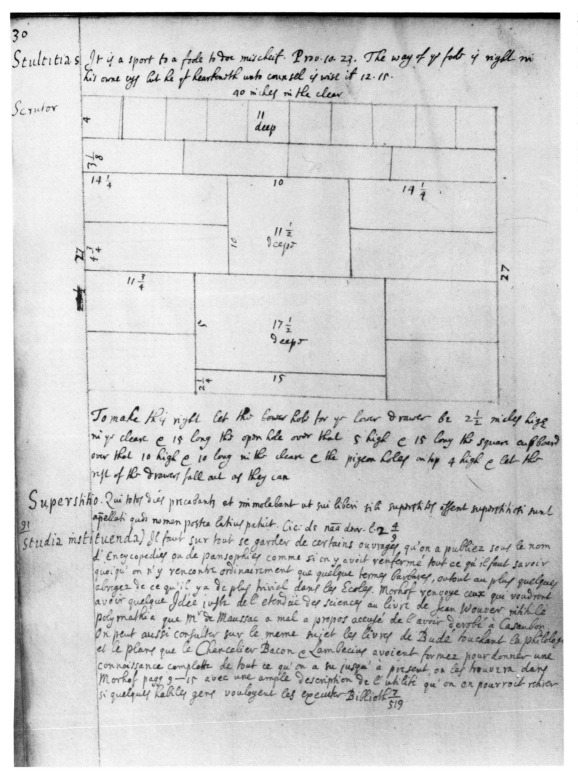

JOHN LOCKE: Autograph notebook containing the earliest known draft of *An Essay concerning Humane Understanding,* and other working notes, 321 pages, 1661-1700
The illustration shows his plan for organizing a desk
Sold 14.6.79 in London for £75,000 ($156,750)
From the collection of Arthur A. Houghton, Jr

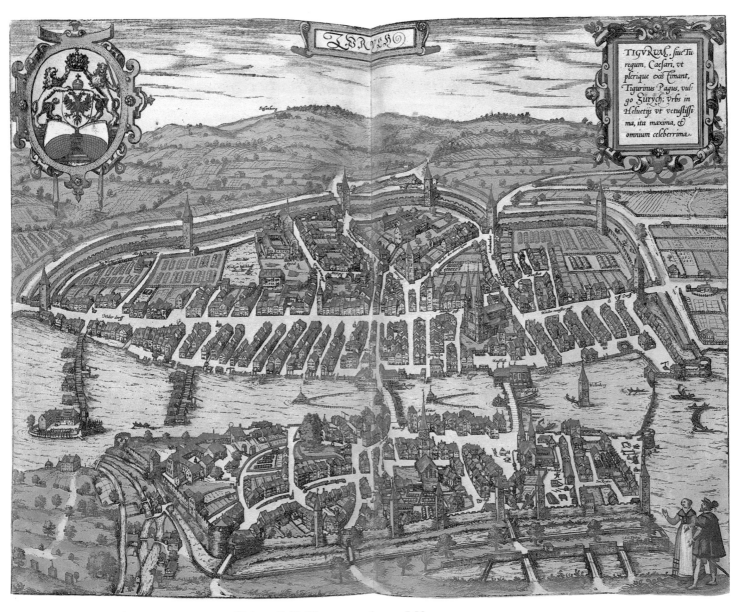

GEORG BRAUN and FRANZ HOGENBERG: *Civitates Orbis Terrarum,* volumes I-V
304 hand-coloured engraved double-page views
Cologne, (1577)-99
Sold 15.11.78 in London for £25,000 ($50,000)

WILLIAM DANIELL and RICHARD AYTON: *A Voyage round Great Britain undertaken in the summer of the year 1813*
308 coloured aquatint plates, 1814-25
Sold 16.5.79 in London for £13,000 ($26,000)

JOAN BLAEU: *Atlas Mayor sino Cosmographia Blaviana*
Nine volumes only (of ten published)
Finely coloured by a contemporary hand, Amsterdam 1658-69
Sold 15.11.78 in London for £44,000 ($88,000)

JOHN GOULD and RICHARD
BOWDLER SHARPE: *A Monograph
of the Trochilidae or Family of
Humming-Birds*
Six volumes with 418 coloured
lithographed plates, 1849-61
and Supplement, 1887
Sold 14.3.79 in London for
£23,000 ($46,000)

JOHN ABBOT and JAMES
EDWARD SMITH: *The
Natural History of the rarer
Lepidopterous Insects of
Georgia*
104 hand-coloured
engraved plates printed
on vellum, 1797
Sold 17.11.78 in New
York for $34,000
(£17,000)
Sold on behalf of Harvard
University, Dumbarton
Oaks Research
Library and Collections

JACOBUS CALCHUS: *Treatise on whether a man may marry the widow of his deceased brother*
Manuscript in Latin, dated 8 April 1530, bound for King Henry VIII by the 'King Henry's Binder' and one of the finest and earliest examples of an English gold-tooled bookbinding
Sold 8.11.78 in London for £60,000 ($120,000)
Record auction price for an English book binding

Biblia Deutsch
The second edition of the Bible
in German, with fine
manuscript decoration
throughout
Strassburg, Heinrich
Eggestein, not after 1470
Sold 27.6.79 in London for
£13,500 ($28,350)

Horae BMV
Book of Hours for the use of Paris
Illuminated manuscript on vellum
with 14 miniatures
Paris, *c.* 1400
Sold 27.6.79 in London for
£26,000 ($54,600)
From the collection of
Mrs Redington Roche

Horae BMV
Book of Hours for the use of
Sarum
Illuminated manuscript in
Latin with sections in English,
full-page miniature and 20
large historiated initials, signed
by the artist
London, *c.* 1425-40
Sold 27.6.79 in London for
£48,000 ($100,800)

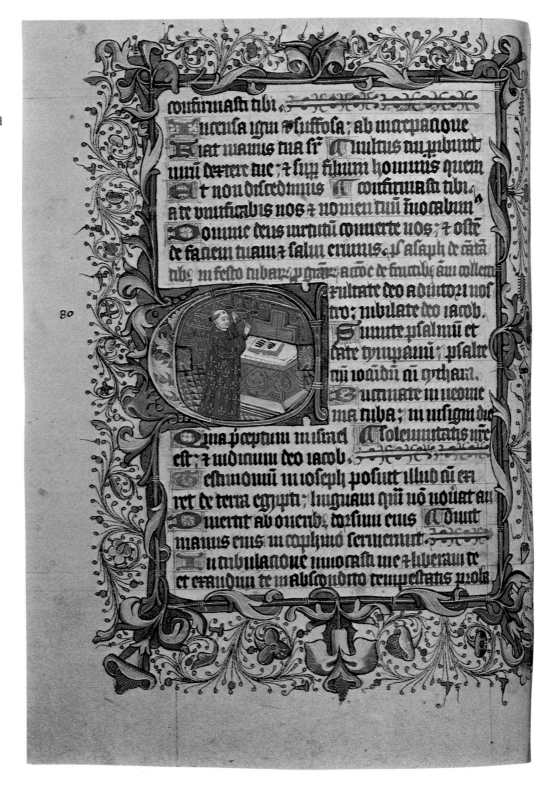

The Richard Wagner Collection formed by the Hon. Mrs Mary Burrell

HANS FELLNER

During the ten years before her death in 1898, the Hon. Mrs Mary Burrell, a wealthy English lady, fired with enthusiasm for Richard Wagner, assembled with much perseverance and determination what became the largest single archive outside Bayreuth of the composer's letters, early works and other memorabilia. She felt that the history of Wagner's life had been seriously misrepresented by his second wife Cosima, and determined to use her newly discovered source to tell the truth in a monumental biography, of which only the first volume, covering the period up to Wagner's 21st year, was published posthumously. The collection was acquired by Mrs Mary Louise Curtis Bok in 1930 and subsequently presented to the Curtis Institute of Music. To be able to maintain the quality of tuition and the policy of scholarships for young musicians, the Institute decided to dispose of the collection. The sale, a unique occasion, took place in New York on 27 October 1978 and attracted enthusiastic Wagnerians from all over the world. The 139 lots realized $1,376,807 (£688,403).

The series of 116 letters from Wagner to his first wife Minna, written between 1835 and her death in 1865, illuminating his passionate courtship and their turbulent marriage, sold for $70,000 (£35,000). The long and profound love letter to Mathilde Wesendonck, written in 1858 and intercepted by Minna, fetched $16,000 (£8,000).

The original manuscripts, however, some of which have never been published, were the high point of the auction. Beginning with a juvenile gothic drama *Leubald,* written when Wagner was only 15, which realized $35,000 (£17,500), the sale continued with an overture and a sonata, both written in 1831, fetching $24,000 (£12,000) and $15,000 (£7,500) respectively. This was followed by his first attempt at opera, the only extant 36-page fragment of *Die Hochzeit,* sold at $36,000 (£18,000). Other early manuscripts included copies of *Die Feen* and *Das Liebesverbot.* Possibly the most significant of all the manuscripts sold was that of *Rienzi,* his first great opera, written and composed between 1837 and 1841, which comprised the original eight-page draft, a subsequent verse draft, the final libretto and the complete 162-page musical composition draft; the whole series realized $150,000 (£75,000). The libretto and stage directions with drawings for *Lohengrin* sold for $95,000 (£47,500), and his unpublished adaptation of Gluck's *Iphigénie en Aulide,* performed in 1847, for $100,000 (£50,000).

As expected, the most hotly contested and highly prized manuscript, at $220,000 (£110,000), was the complete composition draft of the first version of *Tannhäuser,* composed 1843-47, which was preceded by an hitherto unknown small notebook of 1842 containing the earliest prose sketch of the opera, which made $40,000 (£20,000).

It is pleasing to be able to record that most of the significant manuscripts were purchased on behalf of the State Archives at Bayreuth and will continue to be accessible to scholars.

RICHARD WAGNER:
Tannhäuser und der Sängerkrieg auf Wartburg
Autograph manuscript, comprising the composition draft of the opera, 65 leaves, November 1843-April 1847
Sold 27.10.78 in New York for $220,000 (£110,000)
From the collection formed by the Hon. Mary Burrell
Sold on behalf of the Curtis Institute of Music
Record auction price for an operatic manuscript

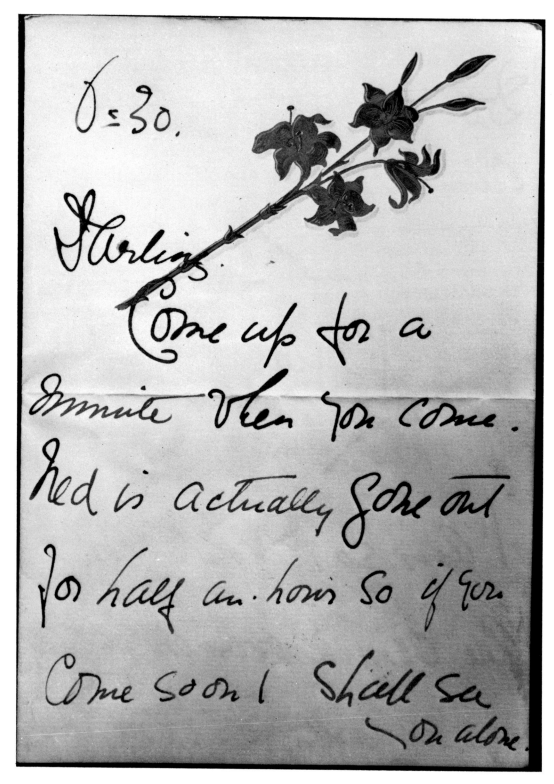

6 = 30.

Darling.
Come up for a
minute when you come.
Ned is actually gone out
for half an hour so if you
come soon I shall see
you alone.

LILLIE LANGTRY: collection of
65 autograph love letters
addressed to Arthur Henry
Jones, her secret lover,
c. 1878-82
Sold 29.11.78 in London for
£8,000 ($16,000)
From the collection of
John Le Gallais, Esq.

FURNITURE AND WORKS OF ART

George III giltwood overmantel
In the manner of Thomas Chippendale
58 × 66 in. (147 × 167.5 cm)
Sold 28.6.79 in London for £17,000 ($35,700)

George III giltwood console table
Designed by Robert Adam and made by William France and John Bradburn
64½ in. (164 cm) wide; 26½ in. (66.5 cm) deep;
34¾ in. (88 cm) high
Sold 30.11.78 in London for £12,000 ($23,400)
This table was made for Sir Laurence Dundas, Bt, in 1765 for the saloon of 19 Arlington Street and passed by descent to the
Marquess of Zetland, by whom it was sold in our rooms 26 April 1934
It is based on a design by Robert Adam dated 1765 and inscribed 'A Table Frame for Long Room next the Eating Parlour' for
which Sir Laurence Dundas was charged 15 guineas

George III mahogany Carlton House writing table
Bearing a label inscribed: This table was made in 1797 for His Royal Highness, The Duke of Clarence, and was presented to his Chaplain, The Rvd. Wm Ellis LL.B from whose family it was purchased
55½ in. (141 cm) wide
Sold 3.2.79 in New York for $28,000 (£14,000)

George III mahogany and marquetry commode
54 in. (137 cm) wide
Sold 22.3.79 in London for £10,000 ($20,000)
The property of Sir Charles Stirling, CMG, KCVO

George III satinwood
and marquetry
cabinet-on-stand inlaid
with English
architectural views
after Buck and ruins
after Clérisseau
40½ in. (103 cm)
wide; 20 in. (51 cm)
deep; 84¼ in.
(213 cm) high
Sold 28.6.79 in
London for £30,000
($63,000)
From the collection of
the Earl of Craven

George III satinwood
'Weekes' secretaire
cabinet
35 ½ in. (90 cm)
wide; 90 ½ in.
(230 cm) high; 22 in.
(56 cm) deep
Sold 28.6.79 in
London for £19,000
($39,900)

George I scarlet
lacquer bureau-
cabinet
41 in. (104 cm) wide;
92½ in. (235 cm)
high; 23 in. (58 cm)
deep
Sold 22.3.79 in
London for £36,000
($72,000)
Formerly in the
collection of Viscount
Kemsley, Dropmore,
Buckinghamshire

Suite of Chinese (Ch'ien Lung) painted wallpaper
126 in. (320 cm) high; 756 in. (1920 cm) long
Sold 30.11.78 in London for £15,000 ($29,250)

The Coates family pair of Queen Anne walnut balloon-seat side chairs
Philadelphia, *c.* 1750-60
Sold 21.10.78 in New York for $160,000 (£80,000)
From the Estate of Elsie C. White
Record auction price for a single lot of American furniture and for any pair of chairs

Chippendale carved mahogany 'triple-top' gaming table
Attributed to John Goddard
Newport, Rhode Island, *c.* 1760-75
28 in. (71 cm) high; 30 in. (76 cm) wide
Sold 21.10.78 in New York for $85,000 (£42,500)

Classical carved mahogany and parcel-gilded marble-top pier table
Attributed to Charles Honoré Lannuier or Duncan Phyfe
New York, *c.* 1815
Sold 5.5.79 in New York for $26,000 (£13,000)

Chippendale mahogany block-front desk or dressing table
Attributed to the Goddard-Townsend family
Newport, Rhode Island, *c.* 1765-75
Sold 21.10.78 in New York for $140,000 (£70,000)
Record auction price for a single piece of American furniture

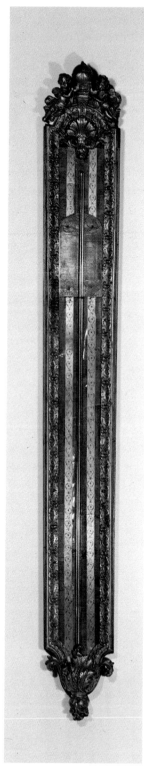

Far left:
Louis XV ormolu and
Sèvres porcelain-
mounted siphon
barometer
c. 1769
The porcelain plaques
with decoration in the
manner of Dodin
26¾ in. (68 cm) high;
10¾ in. (27.35 cm) wide
Sold 9.6.79 in New York
for $50,000 (£24,271)

Left:
Louis XIV ormolu-
mounted tortoiseshell
barometer
47 in. (119.5 cm) high;
5½ in. (14 cm) wide
Sold 7.12.78 in London
for £16,500 ($32,010)

Louis XV ormolu-
mounted lac burgauté
oval panel
16½ × 11½ in.
(42 × 29 cm)
Sold 5.7.79 in London
for £6,000 ($13,440)

Régence Boulle commode
47 in. (119.5 cm) wide; 33¾ in. (86 cm) high; 26½ in. (67 cm) deep
Sold 7.12.78 in London for £16,000 ($31,040)
From the collection of Miss Elizabeth Cartwright, formerly at Aynhoe Park, Northamptonshire

Pair of Louis XV/XVI
giltwood and painted
jardinières
After J.-C. Delafosse
66½ in. (169 cm) high
Sold 18.11.78 in New
York for $38,000
(£19,000)
From the collection of
Mrs Charlotte Ford
Formerly in the Chester
Beatty Collection and
the collection of
Stavros Niarchos

Louis XV black lacquer commode
Probably by F.-A. Mondon
51 in. (129.54 cm) wide
Sold 18.11.78 in New York for $70,000 (£35,000)
From the collection of Mrs Charlotte Ford
Formerly in the collections of Lord Cowper,
A. de Rothschild, Sir Philip Sassoon and Stavros Niarchos

Louis XV/XVI tulipwood and
marquetry coffre à écrire
Attributed to P. Roussel
40 in. (90 cm) high
Sold 18.11.78 in New York for
$75,000 (£37,500)
From the collection of
Mrs Charlotte Ford

Pair of 67 cm terrestrial and celestial globes
By Willem Janszoon Blaeu, 1622
26 ½ in. (67.7 cm) diameter
Sold 5.4.79 in London for £32,000 ($64,000)
Formerly in the collection of the late Lord Egremont, Petworth House
Willem Janszoon Blaeu (1571-1638), the most eminent cartographer of the 17th century, studied astronomy under Tycho Brahe (referred to in a dedication on the celestial globe). He became hydrographer to the Dutch East India Company and in 1633 mapmaker to the Dutch Republic. His business was carried on after his death by his children, whose publications include the celebrated *Grand Atlas*. The 67 cm globes, twice as large as any previously attempted, were his most ambitious projects
Dr Helen Wallis refers to these globes as being acquired by the 9th Earl of Northumberland (1564-1632), 'The Wizard Earl', renowned for his interest in science, and a friend of Sir Walter Raleigh

Florentine pietra dura table top
From the Grand Ducal workshops
Early 17th century
51¼ in. (130 cm) wide; 26 in. (66 cm) deep
Sold 5.7.79 in London for £14,000 ($31,360)

Dresden kingwood petite commode
Mid-18th century
32 in. (81 cm) wide; 32 ½ in. (82.5 cm) high
Sold 18.11.78 in New York for $40,000 (£20,000)

German walnut and marquetry bombe commode
Attributed to the Spindler Brothers
c. 1760-70
48 in. (122 cm) wide
Sold 5.4.79 in London for £36,000 ($72,000)

South German walnut bureau
bookcase
Early 18th century
Sold 21.4.79 in New York for
$50,000 (£25,000)

North German walnut
and marquetry
armoire
Early 18th century
72 ½ in. (184 cm) wide;
25 ½ in. (65 cm) deep;
102 in. (259 cm) high
Sold 30.4.79 for
£19,000 ($38,000)
From the collection of
Bruno Schroder Esq.
and the Schroder
Family
Sold on the premises at
Dell Park, Englefield
Green, Surrey

Rare Flemish feuilles de choux tapestry
16th century
85 × 129 in. (216 × 330 cm)
Sold 14.12.78 in London for £33,000 ($62,700)
From the Mustad Family Collection

Two from a set of four Brussels tapestries from the History of Alexander
By J.F. van der Hecke after designs by Charles Le Brun
Late 17th century
With the arms of the 6th Duke of Veragua
Each panel approx. 159 × 72 in. (409 × 183 cm)
Sold 5.7.79 in London for £19,000 ($42,560)

Willing Seller — Willing Buyer

DESMOND FITZ-GERALD, *The Knight of Glin*

One of the most satisfying aspects of working as Christie's Irish representative is the excitement caused when items of obvious Irish national importance are discovered during my many peregrinations throughout the country. They may not be of any great commercial value but often are of considerable significance from a social-historical as well as an artistic viewpoint. Over the past three years I have arranged a number of 'Willing seller — Willing buyer' sales between private owners and national institutions on both sides of the border.

A modest case in point was an antiquarian and literary notebook of Thomas Lalor Cooke, the historian of Birr, Co. Offaly, dating between 1815 and 1822. Besides his historical jottings, it contains a number of charmingly drawn maps, and views of local towns and antiquities in

Title page from the seventh volume of a set of estate maps (1822-35) of the properties of the 3rd Duke of Leinster by the surveyors Sherrard, Brassington & Greene
Sold by the Duke of Leinster to the National Library of Ireland
Photograph by courtesy of the National Library of Ireland

Triptych attributed to the circle of Jan Prévost
Sold by the Parish of Celbridge for £45,000 ($100,800) to the National Gallery of Ireland
Photograph (before restoration) by courtesy of the National Gallery of Ireland

Offaly. Another is a volume of cooking receipts, medical prescriptions and household hints, compiled by James Burton of Buncraggy, a Clare landlord, living in the early 18th century. It is complete with index, and it gives a fascinating insight into Irish housekeeping of the period. The book is partially a compilation of extracts from other manuals and shows evidence of very wide reading.

More important were seven splendidly bound volumes of estate maps dating from 1822-35, by the Dublin firm of surveyors Sherrard, Brassington & Greene. They chart the Duke of Leinster's manors and lordships in Co. Kildare. There are in all about 150 maps; each volume is decorated with an elaborate title page (see opposite) and the maps themselves have little vignettes showing cottages and features of the various properties. The National Library of Ireland bought all these books, and these maps fill an important gap in the holdings of Leinster material already in their charge.

Irish militaria is of great interest both to the **National Museum of Ireland** in Dublin and to the Ulster Museum in Belfast; the latter has a superb display devoted to local history. Negotiations have included a drum of the Royal Munster Fusileers, used in the 1914-18 War, which went to the National Museum, and a late 18th-century presentation sword (see p.228) inscribed to the Irish patriot James Napper Tandy from the Liberty Volunteers, to the Ulster Museum. The Ulster Museum was also able to buy a set of engraved glass (see p.228) of the Dunluce Infantry, a yeomanry regiment founded in 1795. The glass was probably made by the Belfast Glass Works to commemorate the regiment's disbandment in 1834.

Willing seller — Willing buyer

Late 17th-century black lacquer
Japanese marriage chest
On 18th-century gilt stand
The chest was part of the Restoration
furnishings of Kilkenny Castle
Bought by the Board of Works,
Dublin, for exhibition at Kilkenny
Castle

Detail of the hilt of a presentation
sword
Inscribed: The Gift of the LIBERTY
VOLUNTEERS to Jas Napper
Tandy Esq.
This sword was sold by Napper
Tandy's direct descendant Dr Tandy
Cannon to the Ulster Museum, Belfast

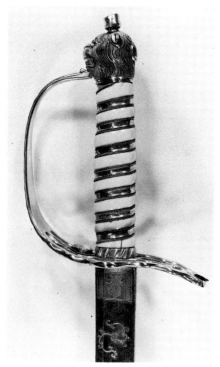

Part of a set of glass of the Dunluce Infantry (formed late in 1795 or early 1796, and
finally disbanded in 1834), comprising two decanters, six rummers and two goblets
Photograph by courtesy of the Ulster Museum, Belfast

228

It is a rarity today in Ireland to be able to trace any of the original pieces of furniture dispersed from Irish collections, so it was something of an occasion when a 17th-century black lacquer Japanese marriage chest (see opposite), catalogued and illustrated in the Ormonde sale at Kilkenny Castle, turned up in a Dublin house. It was probably part of the profusion of lacquer collected by the 1st Duke of Ormonde in the Restoration period and recorded in the many contemporary inventories of the castle. The purchasers, the Board of Works, are returning it to its old home, the newly restored Kilkenny Castle.

Another happy homecoming is the Strokestown travelling carriage or britzska belonging to the Pakenham-Mahon family of Strokestown, Co. Roscommon. The carriage has been long shut up in its coach house but fortunately kept in good condition; for instance, all the white braided interior remains perfect. Mrs Pakenham-Mahon was very pleased to see it sold to her cousin the Hon. Thomas Pakenham, and the coach will be put on display in the stables of Tullynally Castle, Co. Westmeath (formerly Pakenham Hall), the Longfords' huge Gothic revival castle which is now open to the public.

So many owners show great enthusiasm when they know that their treasures will be on view to the general public in a country house, museum or gallery, a further example being the sale for £45,000 ($100,800) of a Flemish early 15th-century triptych attributed, by Gregory Martin of the Picture Department, to the circle of Jan Prévost (see p.227). This has been for many years hidden from view in the parochial house in Celbridge, Co. Kildare. The Diocese of Dublin sanctioned the sale of this picture to the National Gallery of Ireland and it is the most important one that Christie's has negotiated in Ireland so far, but it should be underlined that both great and small often have equal significance in the eyes of history.

The triptych is now being painstakingly cleaned in the conservation department of the Gallery, but our photograph shows it before work had started. Already the canopy above the Virgin and Child has been revealed as a later addition. The donor's identity has not been pinpointed, but his coat of arms should pose no problem. The side panels of St George and St Giles have already come up splendidly. St George has the obligatory Princess in the background, and St Giles's deer that he bandaged in the forest is clearly visible beside the Saint's Abbot's crozier.

Let us hope there will be occasions for many negotiations of the kind we have mentioned, over the years in Ireland, as our museums, galleries and houses open to the public deserve all the support they can get. So much of this nation's heritage has been dispersed that it is a great pleasure to help public bodies and owners in preserving their works of art, books, and objects of national importance so that they remain in this country.

The Master of the Large Foreheads

ROGER PINKHAM, *Victoria and Albert Museum*

The enamel sale of 11 December 1978 was the most important of recent years. It had as its centrepiece twelve enamel plaques painted from Schongauer's *Passion* (B. 9-20) of *c*. 1480.

The artist was the Master of the Large Foreheads (*Maître des Grands Fronts*); he was given that title by Marquet de Vasselot in *Les Emaux Limousins* (Paris, 1921) cat. nos 112-125.

Now it frequently occurs that enamels which originally belonged to a set made from an engraved *Passion* — Dürer's for instance — turn up in the saleroom, for the dismembering of these had started by the early 19th century, if not before; but it is most unusual that the one under discussion has survived intact and in such good condition.

Formally described, the set consists of twelve plaques of uniform dimensions enamelled in schematically arranged colours throughout and counter-enamelled on the reverses in an opaque dark burgundy.

The known provenance of the set goes back to 1882, when it was owned by Ferdinand of Portugal. Subsequently it was in the Wencke and Mannheim Collections until sold by Seligman, New York, in 1908; after that it reappeared in the Anderson Galleries, New York, in 1933, and later was owned by the Vestry of Wye Parish, Maryland, from where it was sent to Christie's last December. There it was bought and lent anonymously to the Victoria and Albert Museum, where it is now on display.

This group attracted critical attention first when shown at the Exposicao Retrospectiva de Arte Ornamental, Lisbon, 1882. Attribution has varied and has not been correct until now. When sold at Seligman's the set was attributed to Jean I Pénicaud, then to his brother Nardon Pénicaud in the sale of 1933. The latter attribution followed Marquet de Vasselot's which, exceptionally, was incorrect, despite his having been the first to catalogue the *oeuvre* of some 25 enamels executed by the Master of the Large Foreheads.

What is known about this artist is not considerable. He was active in the period 1500-25, if not in Nardon Pénicaud's workshop, then close enough to him to be influenced. The MLF is rather a shadowy figure, for unlike Nardon he did not sign or stamp his pieces. Marquet de Vasselot described his manner as impersonal and banal, adjectives which hardly apply to this *Passion* series. Many of the enamels of this artist are single plaques, though he made some triptychs, usually with the *Nativity* scene; so this *Passion* series is his major work in both number of pieces and accomplishment. When seen as a group its outstanding characteristics are the successful projection of Schongauer's taut dramatic sense and the beauty of the colour, particularly the blues.

The essential differences between the styles of Nardon and the MLF lie, first, in the heavier, rounder touch and prevailing melancholy of Nardon's approach, as opposed to a style where

Part of a set of twelve
rectangular Limoges
enamel plaques from
the scenes of the
Passion of Christ
Attributed to the
Master of the Large
Foreheads, after
engravings by Martin
Schongauer
c. 1500
6 ¾ × 4 ⅞ in.
(17 × 12.5 cm)
Later giltwood frames
Sold 11.12.78 in
London for £55,000
($107,800)
Sold on behalf of the
Vestry of Wye Parish,
Maryland, U.S.A.

Christ Harrowing Hell
Engraving by Martin
Schongauer (1450?-91)
from his *Passion* series
of *c.* 1480
Photograph by
courtesy of Dover
Books

Christ Harrowing Hell
Plaque by the Master
of the Large Foreheads
from the series sold
at Christie's

Opposite:
Christ Harrowing Hell
Detail from one of the
plaques on the double
triptych by Nardon
Pénicaud in the
Frick Collection
Early 16th century
Photograph copyright
The Frick Collection,
New York

the enamel is applied more thinly, the touch is more nervous and the body is treated almost skeletally. Additionally the MLF had certain mannerisms which are worth noting when painting physical details, like the large foreheads, the fish-like mouths, heavy-lidded eyes and blade-like noses. When judged from black-and-white photos of the poor quality used in art circles at the beginning of this century, many of the details itemized here were probably hard to read. What are also missing from the black-and-white photos are the differing coloured enamel tones which each of these artists used as a basis on which to paint flesh colour. Nardon employed a greyish white base and on top a lighter warmer white worked in loose geometrical forms; MLF used a pinkish crimson on which he drew neat angular lines and blobs, thinning or thickening the milky tone according to the needs of emphasis. All these points may be seen if this page and the opposite one are compared.

It is worth examining how both artists turned Schongauer's engraving (above left) to their account. This is not so easy as it might appear, for engraving is a linear medium whilst enamelling, like stained glass, deals in coloured fields. The successful transliteration of engraving into enamel is one of the great learned achievements of the Limoges enamellers and one which they managed quickly — in the last quarter of the 15th century. By the early years of the 16th, when both artists were active, the technique had been well established. In the case of the greatest enamellers, what resulted was not only a transliteration but an independent work of art, as in the case of Jean I Pénicaud's treatment of Dürer's engravings. Nardon Pénicaud and the MLF were not artists of great individuality but their work tells us about the technical mastery of their period when the religious zeal of the later Middle Ages was diminishing in France. And in the work of the MLF we can see from his use of Renaissance architectural motifs that he stood at the dividing of the ways, so that he and his contemporaries have in their work a curious but successful blend of Gothic and Renaissance.

Spanish ivory chess
piece
Late 13th century
$3\frac{1}{8} \times 2\frac{1}{4} \times 1\frac{1}{4}$ in.
(7.9 × 6.9 × 3.1 cm)
Sold 9.4.79 in London
for £25,000 ($52,500)
Formerly in the Fuld
Collection, Frankfurt
am Main
A. Goldschmidt
suggests that this lot
might represent one of
two chess pieces: either
the King, since it was
customary in Arabic
chess for that piece to
be represented
uncrowned; or the
Queen, as it is normal
in Arabic plays for
women to be
represented by men.
Weight is added to the
first of these
suggestions by
comparison to
contemporary Arabic
stone carvings

French ivory
rectangular
diptych leaf
14th century
4¼ × 2⅝ in.
(11 × 6.8 cm)
Sold 9.4.79 in London
for £13,500 ($28,350)
Formerly in the
FitzHenry Collection,
sold in our rooms
18 November 1913,
and the
H. Oppenheimer
Collection, sold in our
rooms 15-17 July 1936

Equestrian bronze
figure of
Peter the Great
Attributed to
Pietro Tacca
27 ⅛ in. (69 cm) high;
22 ¾ in. (58 cm) wide
Sold 11.12.78 in
London for £22,000
($43,120)

Bronze figure of Icarus
By Sir Alfred Gilbert, MVO, RA
1884
19⅛ in. (48.5 cm) high
Sold 23.10.78 in London for £12,000
($24,000)
Record auction price for a work by this
artist

Musical Instruments

JAAK LIIVOJA

While the study and appreciation of fine musical instruments is both a challenging and a rewarding subject, the history related to the collecting of these works of art can often be even more fascinating. The social mores which have an undeniable, although not immediately obvious, influence on the craftsman's style can very often be more cogently observed through the eyes of the collector and player. Thus it can be observed that the idea of tradition assumes a justifiably central position in the creative methodology of the individual maker.

The grand pianoforte by Bösendorfer of Vienna, known as the 'Empress Eugénie', presents us with a unique opportunity to observe the skilful combination of elements which, at first glance, appear to be somewhat incompatible. However, by a careful balance of line and ornament in the casework design, Bösendorfer has avoided excesses which could easily have reduced this instrument to the level of caricature.

The 'Eugénie' was commissioned in 1862 by the Empress Elizabeth of Austria as a birthday present for the Empress Eugénie. Work was completed in 1867 and in that year it was exhibited by Bösendorfer at the Paris Exposition Universelle. By the middle of the 19th century the Paris Exhibition had evolved from its inward-looking national beginnings to being flamboyant and international in outlook. In retrospect, the 'Eugénie' was not so much innovative as it was a reflection on the past glories of the 16th and 17th-century art of keyboard instrument manufacture. Bösendorfer had clearly taken great pains to ensure the unity of concept with this remarkable piano. Instead of using the innovative cross-strung frame, he built the instruments around the earlier straight-strung frame. Despite the lavish decoration and the fact that it is fully seven feet long, the 'Eugénie' presents a wonderfully graceful line and a lightness more in keeping with the 18th century than the late 19th. Bösendorfer built very few instruments on this magnificent scale: only the Khedive of Egypt, the Russian Imperial family and the Austrian court possessed comparable pieces.

Domenico Montagnana is today accepted as the greatest luthier of the 18th-century Venetian school. Unfortunately very little is known about this fine maker other than what can be gleaned from his actual instruments. The provenance accompanying the violoncello on p.241 establishes that it was in the possession of the Grand Duke Konstantin Nikolayevich, son of Tsar Nicholas I (1796-1855). It subsequently passed to his son, the Grand Duke Konstantin Konstantinovich. After the death of the latter, his widow the Grand Duchess Elizabeth Mawrievna sold it at the outbreak of the February Revolution and the violoncello eventually found its way out of Russia. The Grand Duke Konstantin Nikolayevich was apparently a fine amateur musician who held regular musical evenings at the Marble Palace, his townhouse in St Petersburg. One of the frequent guests was the great violoncellist Karl Davidoff, who would leave his own Stradivari behind and played instead this Montagnana.

238

The Empress Eugénie
Semi-concert grand piano
By Bösendorfer of Vienna, 1867
Case 84 in. (213 cm) long;
56 in. (147 cm) wide
Sold 14.12.78 in London for £60,000
($114,000)
Record auction price for a 19th-century
piano

Square piano
By Johann Christoph Zumpe, London 1766
Length 47 ¼ in. (120 cm)
Sold 12.6.79 in London for £1,500 ($3,060)
The earliest recorded English-made square piano is by J. C. Zumpe, 1766

Serpent
By Robert Wolf & Co. (London), *c.* 1838
Overall length 100 in. (254 cm)
Sold 8.11.78 in London for £2,000 ($4,000)
Record auction price for a serpent

Violoncello
By Domenico Montagnana
Venice, *c.* 1735
Length of back 29$\frac{1}{16}$ in.
(73.9 cm)
Sold 24.1.79 in London for
£14,000 ($26,600)

Italian violin, by Giovanni Battista Rogeri, Brescia 1703
Length of back 13^{1}⁵/₁₆ in. (35.4 cm)
Sold 12.6.79 in London for £29,000 ($59,160), a record auction price for a violin by this maker

Giovanni Battista Rogeri, born in Bologna about 1650, came under the direct influence of the two great founding schools of Italian violin-making, those of Cremona and Brescia. In 1670, after completing his apprenticeship in Cremona with Nicolo Amati, Rogeri settled in Brescia. Here he produced a uniquely personal model, one which boldly combined the best elements of the Cremonese and Brescian schools. The violin illustrated above is an unusually pure example of this model. At his best, Rogeri was the full equal of the leading makers of the Cremona school, matching the craftsmanship and tonal qualities of Stradivari, Guarneri and Amati

French violin
Attributed to Claude Pierray, Paris, *c.* 1710
Length of back: 14⅜ in. (36.1 cm)
Sold 12.6.79 in London for £4,600 ($9,384)

By the end of the 18th century the French luthiers of Paris and Mirecourt had almost completely adopted the Stradivarius model as their ideal, and consequently a certain degree of individuality was lost in their works. However, in direct contrast, earlier French violins dating from the late 17th and early 18th centuries display an instinctual freedom and spontaneity of concept in design. The violin illustrated above is a fine example of this earlier French school

243

Grande sonnerie striking walnut longcase clock
By Thomas Tompion (and Edward Banger), No. 387, 82 in. (210 cm) high
Sold 18.7.79 in London for £32,000 ($72,640)

This season has seen two exceptional clocks by Tompion at Christie's. The Sussex Tompion dates from before he started to number his clocks. It is probably earlier than his two other clocks extant of this type with square dials of similar layout and two-train grande sonnerie movements embodying a very early application of Barlow's rack-and-snail striking (invented 1676), which made repeating clocks possible. Grande sonnerie striking, whereby the hours and quarters are both struck at each quarter, was but rarely fitted in longcase clocks: only two by Tompion were known, clocks No. 131 and 144. The appearance of a third, No. 387, also provided, through the obscuring of their joint signature by a plaque bearing Tompion's alone, previously recorded on only one clock, No. 292, an unusual insight into the bitter dissolution of his partnership with his nephew, Edward Banger.

Grande sonnerie striking
bracket clock
By Thomas Tompion
14¾ in. (36.5 cm) high
Sold 7.2.79 in London for
£65,000 ($130,000)
From the collection of the
late R.H. Pinder, Esq.
Record auction price for any
English clock

The Sussex Tompion is
illustrated by a number of
authorities and has a
comparatively well-charted
history for a clock. Presented
by the royal clockmaker B. L.
Vulliamy to the Duke of
Sussex, sixth son of George III,
it was sold at Christie's for
£12.10.0 at the dispersal of his
magnificent collection in 1843
Subsequently in Sir John
Prestige's collection, it was sold
in his sale (1963) for £4,300
The price of £65,000
($130,000) on 7 February 1979
was a record on three counts
The longcase clock was
discovered in a house in the
Midlands and had been owned
by that family for about a
century. Its price of £32,000
($72,640) on 18 July 1979 was a
record for a Tompion longcase

Silver-cased carriage
clock with one-minute
tourbillon escapement
and perpetual calendar
Engraved with the
coat-of-arms of the
Prestige family
c. 1900
4⅞ in. (11.5 cm) high
Sold 18.7.79 in
London for £48,000
($108,960)

Japanese clock of
lacquered wood in the
form of a portable shrine
Late 19th century
27 in. (68.5 cm) high
Sold 7.2.79 in London
for £11,000 ($22,000)

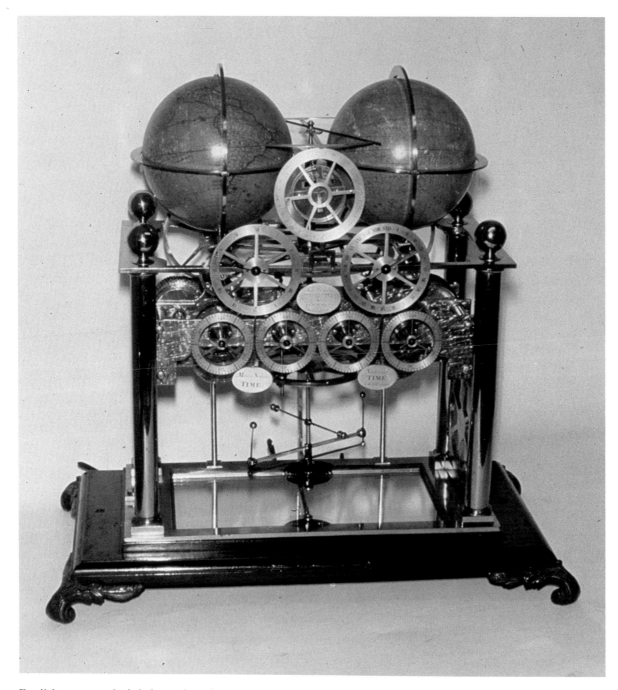

English astronomical skeleton timepiece
By James Gorham, London
With mean and sidereal time indication
27 in. (68.5 cm) high
Sold 7.2.79 in London for £19,000 ($38,000)

Gold hunter-cased
minute-repeating and
grande sonnerie
striking
keyless lever
clockwatch
Signed Parkinson &
Frodsham, nr. 7269
2½ in. (6.35 cm)
diameter
Sold 18.7.79 in
London for £11,500
($25,300)

Gold double-dial astronomical watch
By Jacob Auch
2⅞ in. (7.3 cm) diameter
Sold 8.5.79 in Geneva for Sw. fr. 98,000 (£27,840)

Perpetual calendar equation of time watch
By Patek Phillippe & Cie, No. 111505
2¼ in. (5.8 cm) diameter
Sold 8.5.79 in Geneva for Sw. fr. 135,000 (£38,352)

JEWELLERY

Diamond ring
Set with a pear-shaped diamond
of 15.26 ct
Signed by Harry Winston
Sold 10.5.79 in Geneva for
Sw. fr. 1,000,000 (£284,090)

Centre:
Single-stone diamond ring
Set with a marquise-cut diamond
weighing approximately 9.68 ct
Sold 13.12.78 in New York for
$145,000 (£76,316)
From the Estate of Helen I. Kellogg

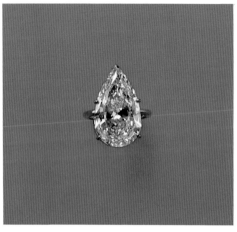

Above:
Diamond ring
Set with a pear-shaped diamond
of 11.19 ct
Sold 10.5.79 in Geneva for
Sw. fr. 450,000 (£127,840)

Above:
Diamond ring
Set with a rectangular-cut diamond
of 19.25 ct
Sold 10.5.79 in Geneva for
Sw. fr. 900,000 (£255,681)

Left:
Step-cut diamond single-stone ring
Weight 12.09 ct approximately
Sold 29.11.78 in London for £125,000
($247,500)
From the collection of the late
Mrs Clare Stillitz

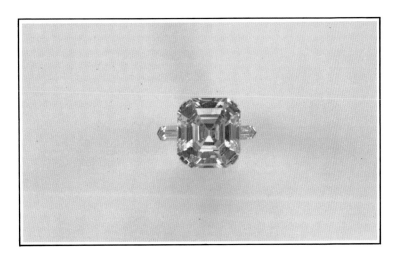

Diamond ring
Set with an emerald-cut light pink
diamond weighing approximately
17.47 ct
Sold 11.4.79 in New York for
$660,000 (£314,285)

Fancy pink diamond ring
Set with a pear-shaped fancy pink
diamond weighing approximately
4.97 ct
Signed by Tiffany-Schlumberger
Sold 13.6.79 in New York for
$305,000 (£148,058)
World record price per carat for
any diamond

Diamond ring
Set with a fancy pink marquise-cut diamond
weighing approximately 20.82 ct
Sold 13.12.78 in New York for $690,000 (£363,158)

Sapphire and diamond
necklace
Total weight of
sapphires 122.30 ct
Total weight of
diamonds 133.78 ct
Signed by
Van Cleef & Arpels
Sold 11.4.79 in New
York for $330,000
(£157,142)
(Illustration slightly
reduced)

Sapphire and diamond
ring
Set with an oval-cut
sapphire weighing
approximately 11.78 ct
Sold 14.2.79 in New
York for $140,000
(£70,000)

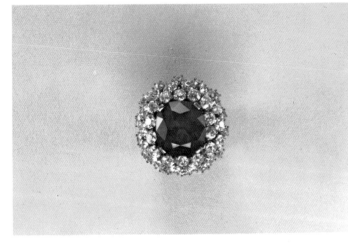

Sapphire and diamond
ring
Set with a cushion-
shaped sapphire of
16.81 ct
Signed by Bulgari
Sold 10.5.79 in
Geneva for
Sw. fr. 200,000
(£56,818)

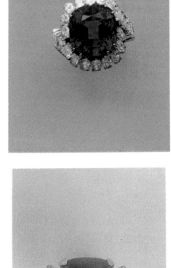

Unmounted cushion-
shaped sapphire of
16.85 ct
Sold 10.5.79 in
Geneva for
Sw. fr. 220,000
(£62,500)

Sapphire bracelet
Signed by Van Cleef & Arpels
Sold 16.11.78 in Geneva for Sw. fr. 280,000 (£86,420)

Cabochon sapphire
and diamond ring
The sapphire of
38.18 ct
Signed by Bulgari
Sold 16.11.78 in
Geneva for
Sw. fr. 550,000
(£169,753)

Art Nouveau pendant
in pliqué-à-jour
enamel
Sold for Sw. fr. 13,000
(£4,012)

Diamond jockey
brooch
Sold for Sw. fr. 4,000
(£1,234)

Antique pearl and
diamond cluster
brooch
Sold for Sw. fr. 8,000
(£2,469)

Enamel and diamond
sliding pocket watch
Signed by Tiffany
Sold for Sw. fr. 11,000
(£3,395)

All sold 16.11.78 in
Geneva

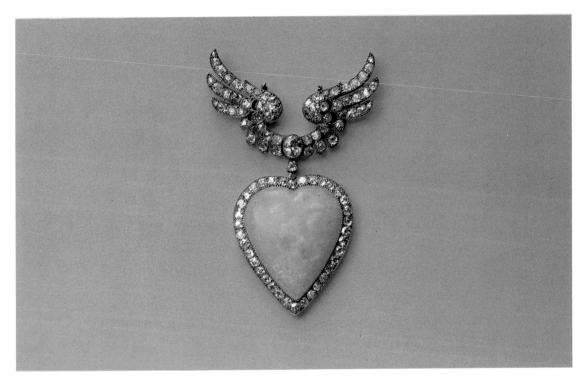

Opal and diamond pendant
Sold 10.5.79 in Geneva for Sw. fr. 20,000 (£5,682)

Pieces of jewellery sent for sale by Christie's in Geneva often have pedigrees attesting to their royal connections. Yet others have come from the collections of the stars of stage, screen and the opera house. Dame Nellie Melba (1859-1931) is a case in point.

The toast of the operatic world, Melba became a legend in her own lifetime and her name a household word; at the height of her career the Australian soprano of Scottish origin was being paid up to $3,000 to sing in *Lucia di Lammermoor* and *Rigoletto* in New York. Feted both in Australia and abroad — Escoffier invented the now-famous *pêche* in her honour — the City of Melbourne celebrated her return in 1910 after an immensely successful three-year tour at the Metropolitan, New York, with a gift of an opal heart set in diamonds by Cartier, which fetched Sw. fr. 20,000 (£5,682) in Geneva last May.

Dame Nellie Melba was apparently untroubled by the legend surrounding a gift of opals, that the wearer of such a stone would die a tragic and premature death. In Melba's case such tragedies were confined strictly to the operatic stage.

Antique ruby and diamond tiara signed by Bolin Moscow
Sold for Sw. fr. 450,000 (£138,889)

All sold 16.11.78 in Geneva

Part of a parure presented by Tsar Alexander II to his daughter
Marie Alexandrowna on the occasion of her marriage in 1874 to
Alfred, Duke of Edinburgh

Opposite:
Antique ruby and diamond ring
Mounted with a cushion-shaped ruby
of 9.19 ct
Sold for Sw. fr. 470,000 (£145,062)

Antique ruby and diamond necklace
Sold for Sw. fr. 1,200,000 (£370,370)

Diamond necklace and
diamond brooch
Signed by
Van Cleef & Arpels
Sold for
Sw. fr. 180,000
(£54,138)

Pair of diamond
ear-clips
Signed by
Van Cleef & Arpels
Sold for Sw. fr. 35,000
(£9,943)

All sold 10.5.79 in
Geneva

Diamond brooch
Signed by Bulgari
Sold 10.5.79 in Geneva for Sw. fr. 270,000 (£76,704)

Ruby and diamond
flower clip
Signed by Van Cleef &
Arpels
Sold for Sw. fr. 27,000
(£7,670)

Ruby and diamond
bracelet
Mounted with
fourteen cushion-
shaped rubies of
38.77 ct within circular
and navette-cut
diamonds of 27.53 ct
Sold for
Sw. fr. 240,000
(£68,182)

Ruby and diamond
brooch
Signed by Van Cleef &
Arpels
Sold for
Sw. fr. 45,000
(£12,784)

All sold 10.5.79 in
Geneva

Ruby and diamond
necklace, bracelet
and ring
Sold for
Sw. fr. 290,000
(£82,386)

Pair of flower cluster
ear-clips en suite
Sold for
Sw. fr. 100,000
(£28,409)

All signed by Van
Cleef & Arpels

All sold 10.5.79 in
Geneva
(Illustration slightly
reduced)

Lavender jade and black onyx desk
clock
Signed Black Starr and Frost. Made
in France
5¼ × 3½ in. (13.3 × 8.8 cm)
Sold for Sw. fr. 60,000 (£18,518)

Marble obelisk clock
Signed Cartier Paris No. 148
Approximately 15⅜ in. (39 cm) high
Sold for Sw. fr. 15,000 (£4,629)

Both sold 16.11.78 in Geneva

Rock crystal, onyx and
agate mystery clock
Signed Cartier Paris
No. 1131, No. 0360
13 ¾ × 9 ½ × 5 ⅛ in.
(35 × 24 × 13 cm)
Sold 16.11.78 in
Geneva for
Sw. fr. 260,000
(£80,246)

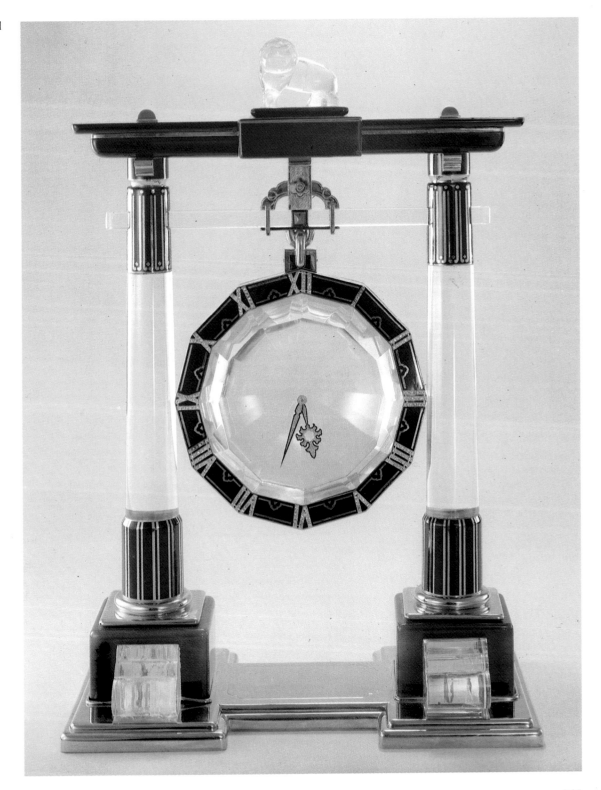

Jade, onyx and gem-set pendant
Made by Cartier in 1921, No. 054
Sold 16.11.78 in Geneva for Sw. fr. 32,000 (£9,876)

Spray of prunus
Signed by Janesich, *c.* 1925
6½ in. (16.5 cm) high
Sold 16.11.78 in Geneva for Sw. fr. 6,000 (£1,851)

Art Deco clock
designed as a Japanese
temple gate
The movement signed
by Vacheron &
Constantin, Nr. 403
144, made for Verger
Frères, Paris, in 1926
Signed by Van
Cleef & Arpels
7 ¾ × 7 in.
(19.5 × 18 cm)
Sold 10.5.79 in
Geneva for
Sw. fr. 650,000
(£184,659)

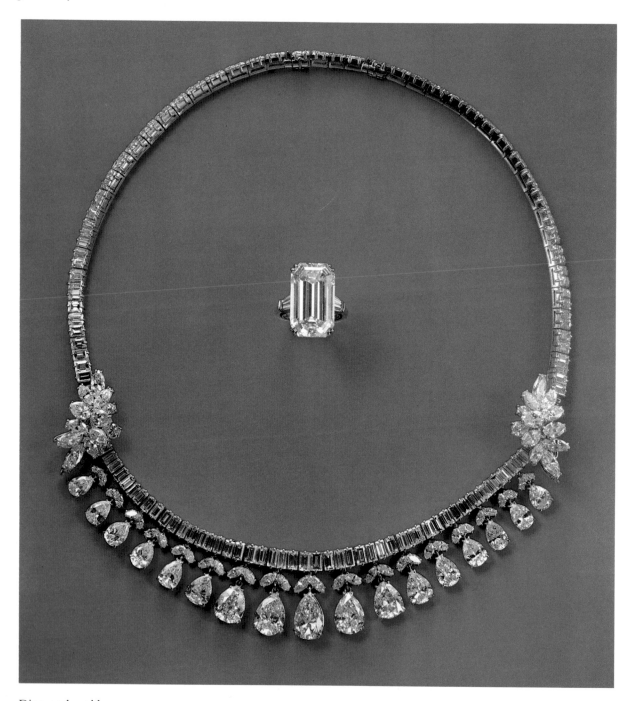

Diamond necklace
Sold for Sw. fr. 220,000 (£62,500)
Diamond ring set with a rectangular-cut diamond of 15.97 ct
Sold for Sw. fr. 600,000 (£170,454)
Both sold 10.5.79 in Geneva

Antique diamond tiara
Sold 10.5.79 in Geneva for
Sw. fr. 420,000 (£119,318)
Given by Queen Victoria to her
daughter Princess Victoria on the
occasion of her marriage in 1838 to
Crown Prince Frederick of Prussia

Pair of diamond ear-pendants
Each suspending a detachable pear-
shaped diamond of 7.60 ct and 7.57 ct
Signed by Van Cleef & Arpels
Sold 16.11.78 in Geneva for
Sw. fr. 850,000 (£262,345)

Antique emerald and
diamond necklace
Sold 16.11.78 in
Geneva for
Sw. fr. 750,000
(£231,481)
(Illustration slightly
reduced)

Emerald and diamond pendant
The oval-cut emerald of 35.77 ct
By Harry Winston
Sold 10.5.79 in Geneva for Sw. fr. 650,000 (£184,659)

Cabochon emerald and diamond brooch
Set with a circular-cut cabochon emerald of 76.24 ct
Signed by Cartier
Sold 16.11.78 in Geneva for Sw. fr. 520,000 (£160,493)

Top:
Antique emerald and
diamond necklace
Sold 16.11.78 in
Geneva for Sw. fr.
300,000 (£92,593)

Henry Wilson jewelled
and enamelled gold
pendant and chain
c. 1905
3¼ in. (8.3 cm)
Sold for £3,800
($7,600)

Moonstone,
chrysolite, enamel and
gold necklace in the
style of Giuliano
Sold for £2,200
($4,400)

Both sold 23.5.79 in
London

Diamond and agate
brooch
By Fabergé
Workmaster August
Holmstrom
Sold for £2,800
($5,516)

Gem-set, pearl,
enamel and gold
necklace and pendant
By Giuliano
Sold for £4,000
($7,880)

Ruby ring
Sold for £8,500
($16,745)

Sapphire ring
Cushion-shaped
sapphire weighing
6.15 ct approximately
Sold for £27,000
($53,190)
From the collection of
Lady Miranda Emmet

All sold 27.9.78 in
London

Art Deco cabochon
ruby, emerald and
diamond lorgnette
Sold for
Sw. fr. 16,000
(£4,938)

Emerald and diamond
bracelet
Sold for
Sw. fr. 23,000
(£7,099)

Art Deco sapphire,
emerald and diamond
pendant fibula
Signed by Cartier
Sold for Sw. fr. 26,000
(£8,025)

Art Deco cabochon
emerald and diamond
brooch
Signed by Boucheron
Sold for Sw. fr. 11,000
(£3,396)

All sold 16.11.78 in
Geneva

Antique ruby,
diamond and pearl
necklace
Sold for £6,800
($13,600)

Emerald and diamond
three-stone half-hoop
ring
Sold for £4,500
($9,000)

Multi-gem ring
Sold for £3,000
($6,000)

Diamond and ruby
brooch
Sold for £1,500
($3,000)

All sold 25.4.79 in
London

Art Nouveau
diamond, gold and
enamel collar
By Lucien Gaillard
Sold 20.6.79 in
London for £21,000
($42,000)

Art Nouveau Jewellery

HANS NADELHOFFER

Art Nouveau in all its forms, be it in London, New York or Geneva, has sold particularly well throughout the year. Outstanding, however, have been the prices realized for two, in many ways similar, pieces of Art Nouveau jewellery with one of them, a choker by René Lalique, selling for a world record auction price of Sw. fr. 170,000 (£48,295).

Figurative jewellery by Lalique is a rare commodity indeed, much more common being works reflecting the artist's passion for plant life. An early piece, the Lalique choker is a joyful combination of the two themes, with a gold-mounted centre motif depicting two wreathed nymphs in shaded grey enamel playing the pan-pipes amidst circular-cut diamond and blue enamel foliage. Its fairyland atmosphere is reminiscent of much of the work of Puvis de Chavannes.

The World Exhibition of 1900 had as one of its main attractions a stand devoted to the work of Lalique, whose output was to influence a whole generation of artists, not least among them being Lucien Gaillard. Already well known for his vases and objects of art, Gaillard was fascinated by his friend's work, particularly in the field of jewellery, and, while not as inventive as his famous mentor, nonetheless produced a number of interesting pieces. One such, a collar, was sold by Christie's in London in June for £21,000 ($42,000).

The collar by Gaillard is composed of three convex rectangular panels, each with sprays of pliqué-à-jour enamelled leaves set with rose diamonds, the gold stems black enamelled, in rose-diamond frames and divided by a diamond bar forming the hinges. As a whole, the piece has about it an air of the stylized lotus leaves of ancient Egypt or the fine India ink designs so beloved of the Chinese and Japanese. From childhood, Gaillard developed a passion for Japanese jewellery and lacquer work which was to have a tremendous impact on the Art Nouveau movement.

276

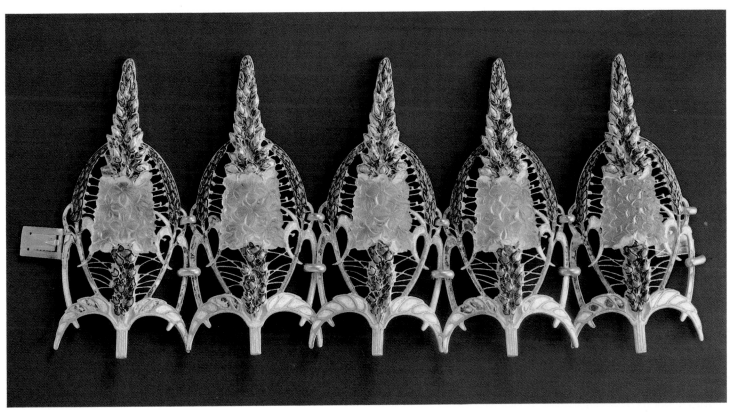

Lalique bracelet
Sold 10.5.79 in Geneva for Sw. fr. 45,000
(£12,784)

Lalique choker
Signed Lalique
Sold 10.5.79 in Geneva for Sw. fr. 170,000
(£48,295)
World record price for a work by Lalique

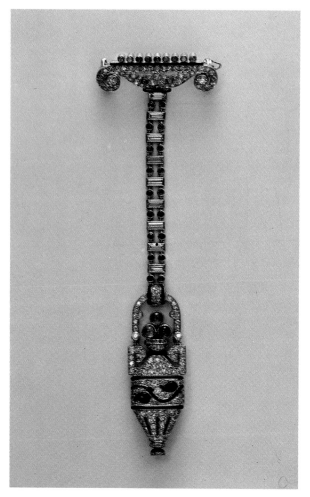

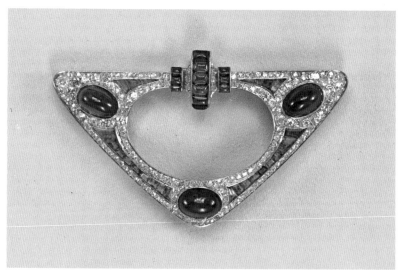

Above:
Art Deco pendant watch
Signed by Lacloche
Sold 16.11.78 in Geneva for Sw. fr. 28,000 (£8,641)

Art Deco sapphire, diamond and black onyx pendant
Signed by Janesitch
Sold 11.4.79 in New York for $20,000 (£9,523)

Art Deco sapphire, emerald and diamond brooch
Sold 14.2.79 in New York for $19,000 (£9,500)

SILVER

Elizabeth I spice-casket
1589
6⅝ in. (16.8 cm) long
Maker's mark TB in script
Sold 22.11.78 in London for £40,000 ($80,000)

Queen Anne ecuelle and cover
By Pierre Platel
London, probably 1706
Overall length 11 in. (28 cm)
Sold 27.9.78 in New York for $13,000 (£6,599)
Sold 21.5.30 in our rooms for £149

Selection of silver-gilt
Sold 21.3.79 in London for £72,800 ($145,600)
From the collection of Lord Camoys

George III gold
standing cup
By Thomas Pitts
1764
15 in. (38.1 cm) high
Sold 21.2.79 in
London for £29,000
($55,100)
From the collection of
the Earl of Craven

Four George II candlesticks
By Paul De Lamerie
1731
9½ in. (24.1 cm) high
Sold 21.2.79 in London for £31,000 ($58,900)
From the collection of the Earl of Craven

Dinner-service
By Paul Storr
1806 and 1807
Sold 21.3.79 in London for £260,000 ($520,000)
Sold by order of the Executors of the late Lord Egremont

This George III dinner-service from Petworth is one of the largest to have appeared on the market, consisting of 185 pieces weighing a total of 6,911 oz., and the price for which it was sold was considerably over double the previous record for a single lot of English silver. The service is engraved with the arms of George, 3rd Earl of Egremont (1751 - 1837), one of the wealthiest noblemen of the period and also one of its greatest art patrons, whose recognition and befriending of artists such as Turner, Constable and Flaxman is well known. In 1801 the Earl married Elizabeth Ilive, by whom he had six illegitimate children prior to their marriage but none subsequent to it that survived infancy. By his consistent reluctance to make a 'suitable marriage', he caused much animosity among those interested parties trying to effect one for him; in 1780, after just such a failure, Horace Walpole described him as 'a most worthless young fellow', though most followed Mrs Delany's epithet of 1794, that 'He is a pretty man, has a vast fortune, and is very generous, and is not addicted to the vices of the times'.

Selection of silver-gilt by Paul Storr
Sold 7.6.79 in New York for $133,000 (£64,563)
From the Christner Collection

Selection of silver by Paul Storr
Sold for $144,000 (£69,903)

Centre front:
Basket by Paul De Lamerie, 1740
Sold for $49,000 (£23,786)

All sold 7.6.79 in New York
From the Christner Collection, which produced a record American total for a silver sale of **$785,880 (£381,495)**

Louis XIV equinoctial dial
Signed I. Chapotot à Paris
c. 1670
Base 4¼ in. (11 cm) square; dial 3¾ in. (9.5 cm)
diameter
Sold 8.5.79 in Geneva for Sw. fr. 80,000 (£22,727)

Four Louis XV table-candlesticks
By Alexis Loir
Paris, 1740
9 ¾ in. (24.8 cm) high
Sold 8.5.79 in Geneva for Sw. fr. 65,000 (£18,466)

Four Louis XIV candlesticks
By François De La Pierre
Paris, 1714
9¼ in. (23.5 cm) high
Sold 14.11.78 in Geneva for Sw. fr. 120,000 (£37,037)

Louis XVI circular tureen, cover and stand
By Claude-Hyacinthe-Nicolas Souchet
Paris, 1787
Diameter of tureen 10 in. (25.5 cm)
Diameter of stand 16 in. (40.5 cm)
Sold 8.5.79 in Geneva for Sw. fr. 62,000 (£17,613)

Louis XIV silver-gilt toilet-service
c. 1675
Sold 8.5.79 in Geneva for Sw. fr. 125,000 (£35,511)

Louis XVIII ormolu
library-lamp
13 ³⁄₈ in. (34 cm) high
Sold 14.11.78 in
Geneva for
Sw. fr. 95,000
(£29,320)

Louis XVI silver-gilt
ecuelle, cover and
stand
By François-Daniel
Imlin
Strasbourg, 1781
Diameter of stand
10 in. (25.5 cm)
Sold 8.5.79 in Geneva
for Sw. fr. 35,000
(£9,943)

Parcel-gilt tankard
German or
Transylvanian
c. 1575
7 in. (18 cm) high
Sold 14.11.78 in
Geneva for
Sw. fr. 38,000
(£11,728)

Paul van Vianen Plaque

T.MILNES GASKELL

The discovery of this plaque, which before its identification was thought to have been lost and only known to have existed through the electrotype of 1845 by B. Holz in the collection of Count von Furstenberg at Schloss Heiligenberg, aroused considerable interest throughout Europe when sold by us on 21 March. Its creator, Paul van Vianen, both artist and goldsmith, was appointed in 1603 to the Imperial court workshop of Rudolph II in Prague and remained there until his death in 1613 or 1614. He is generally accredited as being the pre-eminent goldsmith at the court, and this piece displaying remarkable technical virtuosity lends credence to this view, especially as the corpus that remains of his work is limited. It is probably that the design of this plaque is his own and it is interesting to note that the figures are dressed in contemporary costume.

Opposite:
Silver plaque
By Paul van Vianen
Signed with monogram PV and dated 1607
12½ × 9 in. (31.8 × 22.9 cm)
Sold 21.3.79 in London for £75,000 ($150,000)
From the collection of Miss Jane Starkey
World record price for a piece of silver by Paul van Vianen

Parcel-gilt figure of the infant Bacchus
By Hans Lambrecht III
Hamburg, *c.* 1650
25 ¾ in. (65.5 cm) high
Sold 14.11.78 in Geneva for
Sw. fr. 180,000 (£55,555)

German silver-gilt
model of a lion
17th century
12 in. (30.5 cm) high
Sold 28.3.79 in New
York for $16,500
(£8,250)

Eight from a set of sixteen candlesticks
By Johann Wilhelm Voigt I
Osnabrück, *c.* 1725
8¼ in. (20.9 cm) high
Sold 14.11.78 in Geneva for Sw. fr. 165,000 (£50,925)

OBJECTS OF ART
AND VERTU

Top:

JOHN SMART: *A Lady*
Signed with initials, dated 1804
3 in. (7.6 cm) high
Sold 27.3.79 for £5,200 ($10,920)

CHARLES SHERRIFF: *A Gentleman*
$2\frac{5}{8}$ in. (6.7 cm) high
Sold 27.3.79 for £1,400 ($2,800)

Centre:

GEORGE ENGLEHEART: *A Gentleman*
$1\frac{7}{8}$ in. (4.8 cm) high
Sold 27.3.79 for £1,700 ($3,400)

RICHARD CROSSE: *A Girl*
$1\frac{1}{2}$ in. (3.8 cm) high
Sold 26.6.79 for £1,200 ($2,520)

Bottom:

JOHN BOGLE: *A Continental Officer*
Signed and dated 1792
$2\frac{1}{8}$ in. (5.4 cm) high
Sold 26.6.79 for £2,600 ($5,460)

RICHARD CROSSE: *Edward or James Crosse*
4 in. (10 cm) high
Sold 28.11.78 for £5,500 ($10,890)

RICHARD COSWAY: *The Hon. Mrs Damer*
Signed with monogram and on the reverse and dated 1785
2⅜ in. (6.1 cm) high
Sold 28.11.78 for £3,800 ($7,524)
Now in the National Portrait Gallery

ALEXANDER COOPER: *William, Lord Craven*
Signed with initials
1⅜ in. (3.5 cm) high
Sold 26.6.79 for £6,500 ($13,650)

SUSAN PENELOPE ROSSE, after SAMUEL COOPER: *Cosimo III*
3⅜ in. (8.8 cm) high
Sold 27.3.79 for £5,500 ($11,000)
From the collection of the Lord Clifford of Chudleigh, OBE, DL

RICHARD COSWAY: *A Lady*
2¾ in. (7 cm) high
Sold 26.6.79 for £5,000 ($10,500)

All sold in London

303

Gold boxes

Louis XV enamelled burnished gold snuff-box
By Jean-François Garand
Paris, 1754
3 in. (7.7 cm) long
Sold 8.5.79 in Geneva for Sw. fr. 170,000
(£48,295)

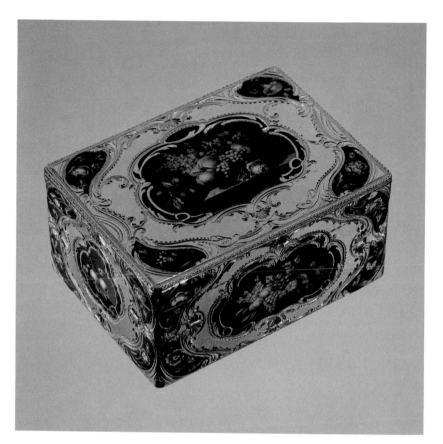

George II enamelled gold snuff-box
By James Bellis
2⅜ in. (6 cm) long
Sold 8.5.79 in Geneva for Sw. fr. 95,000 (£26,988)

Swiss enamelled gold butterfly-box
Geneva, early 19th century
2⅞ in. (7.3 cm) wide
Sold 27.3.79 in London for £9,000 ($18,000)

Above:
Swiss gold snuff-box
c. 1800
3 ¼ in. (8.3 cm) long
Sold for £4,200 ($8,316)

Louis XV vari-coloured gold snuff-box
By Nicolas Marguerit
Paris, 1777
3 ⅛ in. (8 cm) long
Sold for £5,500 ($10,890)

Both sold 28.11.78 in London

Louis XV vari-coloured gold snuff-box
By Jean-François Defer
Paris, 1765
3 ⅜ in. (8.5 cm) long
Sold 8.5.79 in Geneva for Sw. fr. 65,000 (£18,465)

Oval gold snuff-box
The cover painted with a
coat-of-arms, motto and
supporters by Bernard Lens
c. 1715
3¼ in. (8.3 cm) long
Sold 26.6.79 in London for
£14,000 ($29,400)

French diamond-encrusted
gold snuff-box
By Gabriel-Raoul Morel
The cover with miniature of
Queen Maria Cristina of Spain
by Florentino De Craene
Paris, 1819-38
3½ in. (9 cm) long
Sold 28.11.78 in London for
£20,000 ($39,600)
From the collection of
M. D. Llewellyn, Esq.

Top:
George II gold-
mounted mocha agate
snuff-box
18th century
2 ¾ in. (7 cm) wide
Sold for £2,000
($3,960)

Left:
Louis XV gold
pocket-telescope
1762-8
2 ½ in. (6.5 cm) high
Sold for £1,400
($2,772)

George II gold
snuff-box *c.* 1740
1 ¾ in. (4.5 cm) wide
Sold for £2,700
($5,346)

Centre:
Louis XV enamelled
gold etui *c.* 1750
4 in. (10 cm) high
Sold for £5,500
($10,890)

Right:
George III
gold-mounted
bloodstone etui
c. 1770
3 ½ in. (9 cm) high
Sold for £1,600
($3,168)

Bottom:
Gold-mounted
mother-of-pearl
snuff-box
c. 1715
3 ⅛ in. (8 cm) long
Sold for £2,300
($4,554)

All sold 28.11.78 in
London

Selection of objects of
vertu, including a
carved ivory ring
and a diamond-set
ring-watch, gold and
silver fob-seals,
serpent jewellery
and gold-mounted
stick-pins
Sold individually
27.3.79 in London for
£10,650 ($21,300)

George III gold-mounted agate necessaire
Unmarked but signed on the wood lining: J.(?) Barbot, London, fecit 1765
$2\frac{7}{8}$ in. (7.3 cm) high
Sold 28.3.79 in New York for $10,000 (£5,000)

Documentary German jewelled and enamelled gold-mounted agate bowl and cover
Unmarked, but by Reinhold Vasters
Aachen, *c.* 1870
Overall length 19 in. (48.2 cm); height 13 ¼ in. (33.6 cm)
Sold 28.3.79 in New York for $60,000 (£30,000)

A collection of Russian
miniature Easter eggs
Sold individually 15.11.78 in
Geneva for a total of
Sw. fr. 53,300 (£16,450)

Gold-mounted
jewelled nephrite
frame
Signed
Workmaster
Fedor Afanassiev
St Petersburg
1899-1908
2½ in. (6.5 cm) high
Sold for Sw. fr. 14,000
(£4,321)

Jewelled and
gold-mounted nephrite
frame
Signed
Workmaster
Hjalmar Armfelt
St Petersburg
1899-1908
3⅜ in. (8.5 cm) high
Sold for Sw. fr. 20,000
(£6,173)

Enamelled gold and
silver-gilt frame
Signed
Workmaster
Viktor Aarne
St Petersburg
1899-1908
2¾ in. (7 cm) high
Sold for Sw. fr. 10,000
(£3,086)

Orange striated
carnelian figure of a
squirrel
2⅛ in. (5.5 cm) long;
1⅝ in. (4.2 cm) high
Sold for Sw. fr. 35,000
(£10,802)

All by Fabergé
All sold 15.11.78
in Geneva

Gold-mounted and
enamelled jewelled
silver cigarette case
Signed
Workmaster
August Hollming
St Petersburg
1899-1908
3⅞ in. (9.8 cm) long
Sold for Sw. fr. 9,000
(£2,777)

Enamelled silver-gilt
clock
Signed
Workmaster
Michael Perchin
St Petersburg, late
19th century
5⅝ in. (14.3 cm) high
Sold for Sw. fr. 17,000
(£5,247)

Both by Fabergé
Both sold 15.11.78 in
Geneva

Gem-set silver-gilt and shaded cloisonné enamel presentation dish with grisaille views of Moscow
Signed with the initials of Fabergé and Fedor Rückert
Moscow, *c.* 1907
5⅞ in. (15 cm) diameter
Sold for Sw. fr. 19,000 (£5,397)

Presentation beaker en suite
Stamped with the Imperial Warrant mark of Fabergé Workmaster Fedor Rückert
Moscow, 1899-1908
4 in. (10.2 cm) high
Sold for Sw. fr. 17,000 (£4,829)

Both sold 9.5.79 in Geneva

French ivory chess-set,
featuring Napoleon
and the Austrian
Emperor Francis
Height of Kings
4 ¼ in. (10.8 cm);
height of pawns
3 ¼ in. (8.4 cm)
Sold 18.6.79 in
London for £1,700
($3,570)

Madras papier-mâché
chess-set
Late 18th century
Height of Kings 4 in.
(10.5 cm); height of
pawns 2 in. (5.2 cm)
Sold 18.6.79 in
London for £1,600
($3,360)

Both from the
collection of Amos
Smith, Esq.

St John the Baptist
Greek, 16th century
31 ¾ in. (85.8 cm) high
Sold 17.10.78 in London for £4,500 ($9,000)

The Archangels Michael and Gabriel
Greek, late 16th/early 17th century
11 ½ in. (29.2 cm) high
Sold 17.10.78 in London for £5,000 ($10,000)

Triptych
Central Russian, 18th century
16 ¼ in. (46.4 cm) high; width when opened
23 ¼ in. (59 cm)
Sold 17.10.78 in London for £3,000 ($6,000)

Icon of St Nicholas
North Russian, late 16th
century
26¼ in. (66.7 cm) high
Sold 28.2.79 in London for
£6,500 ($12,350)

St Demetrios of Thessalonica
Macedonian, 17th century
38¾ in. (98.4 cm) high
Sold 17.10.78 in London for
£13,000 ($26,000)

Opposite:
Icon of the Presentation of the
Virgin Mary in the Temple
By Fedor Rückert
Moscow, 1896-1908
12½ × 11 in. (31½ × 28 cm)
Sold 27.4.79 in New York for
$75,000 (£36,764)
World record price for an icon
sold at auction

Lieutenant General Sir William Stewart's Peninsular Gold Cross Group

R.SANCROFT-BAKER

Lieutenant General Sir William Stewart was born on 10 January 1774, the second son of the 7th Earl of Galloway. He received a commission as ensign in the 42nd foot on 8 March 1786, became lieutenant in the 67th foot on 14 October 1787, and captain of an independent company on 24 January 1791. He was wounded in the unsuccessful attempt on Pointe-à-Pitre on 2 July 1794, when Guadeloupe had been recovered by the French. He returned to England in November and obtained a majority in the 31st foot.

Stewart was made lieutenant-colonel in the army and assistant adjutant-general to Lord Moira's corps on 14 January 1795, and in June he served on the staff of the expedition to Quiberon. On 1 September he was given command of the 67th foot, and went with it to San Domingo. Returning to Europe he obtained leave to serve with the Austrian and Russian armies in the campaign of 1799 and was present at the battle of Zurich. It was probable that what he saw of Croats and Tyrolese in this campaign led him to propose, in concert with Colonel Coote Manningham, that there should be a corps of riflemen in the British army. The proposal was adopted and an experimental 'corps of riflemen' was formed in January 1800. In August of that year he went with three companies of his rifles to Ferrol in Pulteney's expedition and was badly wounded in the first skirmish. He commanded the troops who served as marines in the fleet sent to the Baltic in 1801. He was on board Nelson's flagship at Copenhagen. Later Nelson, writing to St Vincent, described him as 'the rising hope of the army' and a lasting friendship ensued: by Nelson's wish Stewart's son was named Horatio.

He was promoted major-general on 25 April 1808 and on 31 August 1809 he was made colonel of the 3rd battalion of the corps he had formed, the 95th rifles. He was sent to the Peninsula in 1810 to command the British and Portuguese troops which were to form part of the garrison at Cadiz. In August 1812 he returned again with the local rank of lieutenant-general. At Vittoria he was on the right under Hill, who spoke highly of his conduct. He was included in the thanks of Parliament and was made KB on 11 September. He was popular with the men of his division, among whom he was known as 'auld grog Willie' on account of the extra allowances of rum which he authorized, and which Wellington made him pay for! For his service in the Peninsula he received the Gold Cross with two clasps, the Portuguese Order of the Tower and Sword, and the Spanish Order of San Fernando. On 2 January 1815, on the enlargement of the Order of the Bath, he received the GCB. He had been MP for Saltash in 1795 and for Wigtonshire from 1796 until he retired in 1814 on account of ill health, which was not surprising after seventeen campaigns. In July 1818 he was transferred to the colonelcy of the 1st battalion of what had then become the rifle brigade. He settled at Cumloden on the borders of Wigton and Kirkcudbrightshire near the family seat. He died there on 7 January 1827.

Peninsular Gold Cross group awarded to Lt. Gen. Sir William Stewart, GCB (1774-1827)
Sold 18.4.79 for £26,000 ($54,600)
Record auction price for a named group of orders and decorations

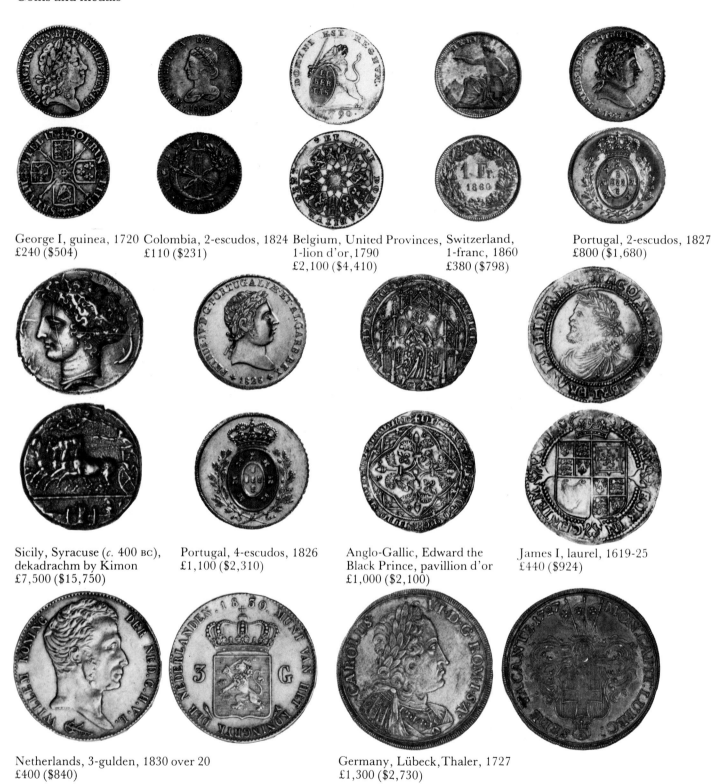

George I, guinea, 1720
£240 ($504)

Colombia, 2-escudos, 1824
£110 ($231)

Belgium, United Provinces,
1-lion d'or, 1790
£2,100 ($4,410)

Switzerland,
1-franc, 1860
£380 ($798)

Portugal, 2-escudos, 1827
£800 ($1,680)

Sicily, Syracuse (c. 400 BC),
dekadrachm by Kimon
£7,500 ($15,750)

Portugal, 4-escudos, 1826
£1,100 ($2,310)

Anglo-Gallic, Edward the
Black Prince, pavillion d'or
£1,000 ($2,100)

James I, laurel, 1619-25
£440 ($924)

Netherlands, 3-gulden, 1830 over 20
£400 ($840)

Germany, Lübeck, Thaler, 1727
£1,300 ($2,730)

Russia, Sophia Alexievna,
2-ducats
£1,200 ($2,520)

Russia, 5-roubles,
1803, unique
£3,000 ($6,300)

Russia, pattern 10-roubles, 1836
£5,500 ($11,550)

Poland, 3-roubles/20-zlotych,
1841, unique
£3,000 ($6,300)

Poland, pattern 2-zlotych,
1818
£2,000 ($4,200)

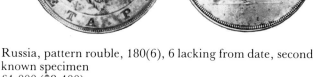

Russia, pattern 1½-roubles, 1835
£7,000 ($14,700)

Russia, pattern rouble, 180(6), 6 lacking from date, second
known specimen
£4,000 ($8,400)

All sold in London

The above seven coins are from the collection sold on 15 June 1979 for a total of £168,548 ($353,951). Most of the coins
were collected in St Petersburg in the years before the Revolution. Many of the rarer specimens were acquired from the
leading collectors of the day, some of whose names are not well known in the West. Among the foremost were Count
Bobrinsky, Baron Nolken and Scrobatov. The collection was added to in the years between the Revolution and the
Second World War, notable specimens being purchased at the Soviet Government's auctions held in Germany between
1927 and 1932. Most of the coins from the Count Ivan Tolstoi, Grand Duke Georgii Michailovich and Count Emeric
Hutton-Czapski collections were added during these years. The sale included at least two unique coins and many
exceptional rarities, of particular note being the 5-roubles, 1803 (said to have been presented by Alexander I to one of
the greatest of Russian numismatists, Count Ivan Tolstoi), the 3-roubles or 20-zlotych, 1841 of St Petersburg mint from
the collection of Grand Duke Georgii Michailovitch, and the pattern rouble of 1806 with the obverse die unfinished. The
last coin is the second known specimen, the other being in the Hermitage collection in Leningrad. The pattern imperial
of 15-russ was one of only five known and it was the first time that the rare patterns of 1911 (in nickel) and 1916 were
offered for sale in the West

Prussia, Order of the
Black Eagle, gold and
enamel Grand Cross
Badge and Collar
By Hossauer of Berlin
Sold 14.11.78 in
Geneva for
Sw. fr. 75,000
(£23,148)

CERAMICS AND GLASS

Pair of Worcester (Dr
Wall) candlesticks
c. 1760
10¼ in. (26 cm) high
Sold 14.5.79 in
London for £14,500
($29,000)

Chelsea group,
The Music Lesson
c. 1765
Gold anchor mark
15 ½ in. (39.5 cm)
high
Sold 8.6.79 in
New York for
$11,000 (£5,339)
From the
Christner Collection

Pair of Rockingham
plates
c. 1826/30
9¼ in. (23.5 cm)
diameter
Sold 27.11.78 in
London for £1,300
($2,574)

Chelsea fable-decorated plate,
The Lion that was Sick
Painted by Jeffryes Hamett O'Neale
c. 1752
8⅞ in. (22.5 cm) diameter
Sold 11.6.79 in London for £2,400 ($4,800)

London decorated Nantgarw plate
c. 1816
9¾ in. (24.8 cm) diameter
Sold 27.11.78 in London for £2,000 ($3,960)

Staffordshire coloured saltglaze figure
of a hawk
1755
7¼ in. (18.5 cm) high
Sold 4.6.79 in London for £6,500
($13,000)

Liverpool (William Reid)
blue and white figure of a
dismal hound
c. 1756
1¾ in. (4.5 cm) high
Sold 11.12.78 in London
for £1,000 ($1,960)
From the collection of the
Hon. Mrs Cayzer

Liverpool (Christian's)
blue and white inscribed
and dated inkpot
3⅛ in. (8 cm) wide
Sold 11.12.78 in London
for £1,100 ($2,156)
From the collection of
Mrs R.M. Roberts

London Delft blue and
white figure of a seated
cat
c. 1680
4¼ in. (10.8 cm) high
Sold 29.1.79 in London
for £4,000 ($7,600)
Sold by order of the
Trustees of the
late Countess Temple
of Stowe

Lambeth Delft blue and
white dated oval pill-slab
1687
11¾ in. (30 cm) high
Sold 29.1.79 in London
for £5,000 ($9,500)
Sold on behalf of the
Trustees of the Swithland
Settled Estates

Pair of Wedgwood and Bentley blue and white jasper rectangular plaques *c.* 1778
From the John Augustus Tulk Collection
Sold by order of the Governors of Sir William Perkins' Educational Foundation
Impressed upper-case marks
6¼ × 15¾ in. (16 × 40 cm)
Sold 25.9.78 in London for £7,500 ($14,775)

Not Without Lustre

HUGO MORLEY-FLETCHER

Both sides of the Atlantic this year saw remarkable examples of early Spanish and Italian pottery which stimulated high prices.

In New York in April a splendid Hispano-Moresque armorial dish, datable *c.* 1430 and formerly in the Prussian Royal Collection and that of William Randolph Hearst, was sold after heated bidding between three European contenders for $60,000 (£30,000), certainly a record price in the United States for a piece of the kind.

2 July in London saw a wide range of early Italian pieces from all the major factories active in the 16th century. The top price of £32,000 ($70,080) was paid twice, for a Gubbio lustred armorial dish, which in 1935 had fetched £609 in the Burns sale at Christie's; and for a Castel Durante tondino by Zoan Maria, which when it last appeared at Christie's in 1899 from the Richard Zschille, Grossenheim, Dresden sale, fetched £270. A large Faenza (Casa Pirota) dated istoriato berretino dish, which in the Pringsheim sale in 1939 sold for £90, now fetched £30,000 ($65,700). Another lustred piece, a tondino from Gubbio, last sold at Christie's in 1925 in the Humphrey W. Cook sale for 650 guineas, now brought £14,000 ($30,660). An unrecorded Caffaggiolo tondino with the Medici arms and fully marked on the back, strangely omitted from all the literature of the subject, brought £23,000 ($50,370), whilst £17,000 ($37,230) was paid for a Gubbio lustred istoriato dish dated 1539, notable for the strength and brilliance of the polychrome decoration. The sale also included a series of seven Deruta lustred dishes, five of which had passed through the London rooms in the 19th century; these ranged in price from £5,500 to £11,000 ($12,045 to $24,090), the last amount doubling the highest price paid at auction for wares of this type.

All the above pieces were noteworthy for their very clean condition and it is clear that in the realm of early European pottery fine condition, preferably attached to a good, or better distinguished, provenance, adds the essential lustre to the price.

Castel Durante blue-ground tondino
By Zoan Maria
c. 1510
10⅝ in. (27 cm) diameter
Sold 2.7.79 in London for £32,000 ($70,080)
From the collection of Joseph Homberg
Sold on behalf of Jacques Homberg

Gubbio lustred armorial tondino
c. 1525
10⅝ in. (27 cm) diameter
Sold 2.7.79 in London for £32,000 ($70,080)
From the collection of Joseph Homberg
Sold on behalf of Jacques Homberg

Faenza (Casa Pirota) dated istoriato berretino dish
Dated 1537
18½ in. (47 cm) diameter
Sold 2.7.79 in London for £30,000 ($65,700)

Hispano-Moresque gold and copper lustre
armorial dish (front and back views)
Valencian, early 15th century
17⅝ in. (44.8 cm) diameter
Sold 21.4.79 in New York for $60,000
(£30,000)

Caffaggiolo blue and white armorial tondino
Lustred at Gubbio
c. 1510
Blue SPF monogram mark
8⅞ in. (22.5 cm) diameter
Sold 2.7.79 in London for £23,000 ($50,370)

Urbino istoriato dish
Painted by Francesco Xanto Avelli and lustred at Gubbio by Maestro Giorgio Andreoli
Dated in copper-lustre 1539 and inscribed in blue: Del bon tideo et polo/nice
10¾ in. (27.5 cm) diameter
Sold 2.7.79 in London for £17,000 ($37,230)

Deruta blue and gold lustre charger
c. 1520
16⅞ in. (43 cm) diameter
Sold 2.7.79 in London for £12,000 ($26,280)

Dutch Delft armorial
part service
c. 1760
Sold 25.6.79 in
London for £24,450
($51,345)
From the Battle Abbey
Settled Estates

Opposite:
Strasbourg faience
figure of
L'Abbé de Cour
1745-8
13 in. (33 cm) high
Sold 5.2.79 in London
for £11,500 ($23,000)

Zurich figure of a lady
skating
Modelled by
J.W. Spengler
c. 1773
5½ in. (14 cm) high
Sold 17.11.78 in
Geneva for
Sw. fr. 10,000
(£3,086)

Opposite
Meissen group of the indiscreet Harlequin
Modelled by J. J. Kändler
c. 1740
Traces of blue crossed swords mark
6½ in. (17 cm) high
Sold 8.6.79 in New York for $42,000 (£20,388)
From the Christner Collection

Selection of Meissen birds
Sold 25.6.79 in London for a total of
£63,900 ($134,190)

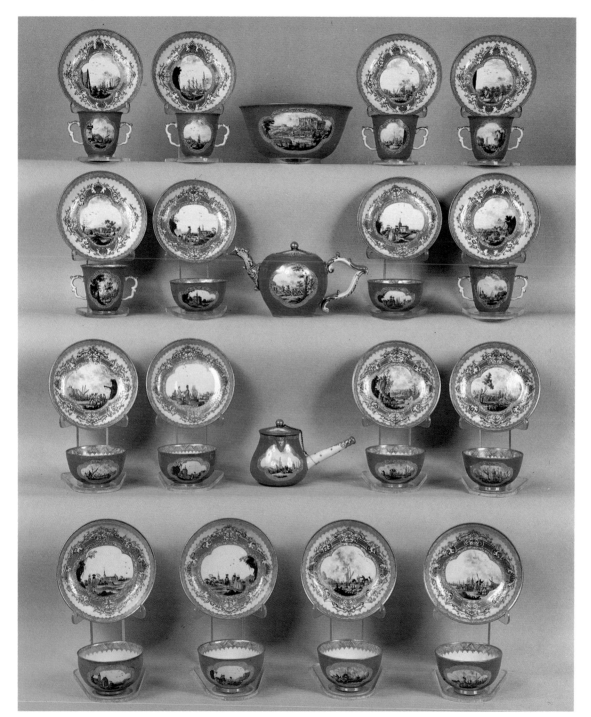

Selection of Meissen powdered purple-ground porcelain
Sold 25.6.79 in London for a total of £34,200 ($71,820)

Meissen sleigh group
Modelled by J. J. Kändler
c. 1741
12¼ in. (31 cm) long
Sold 17.11.78 in Geneva for Sw. fr. 50,000 (£15,432)

Vincennes
turquoise-ground
pear-shaped ewer and
shaped oval basin
c. 1753
The ewer 7 ½ in.
(19 cm) high; the basin
11 ¼ in. (28.5 cm)
wide
Sold for Sw. fr. 22,000
(£6,250)

Vincennes
yellow-ground
plateau de moutardier
ordinaire
c. 1752
7 in. (18 cm) wide
Sold for Sw. fr. 8,000
(£2,272)

Vincennes ewer and
cover
c. 1750
7 ½ in. (19 cm) high
Sold for Sw. fr. 26,000
(£7,386)

All sold 7.5.79 in
Geneva

Meissen and Louis XV gold-mounted snuff-box
Painted after J. P. Rugendas
c. 1740
The mounts struck twice with décharge
2 ¾ in. (7 cm) high
Sold 25.6.79 in London for £11,000 ($23,100)

Meissen beaker vase
Painted by J. E. Stadler
c. 1730
Blue crossed swords mark
5 ¼ in. (13.5 cm) high
Sold 4.12.78 in London for £7,000 ($13,580)

Würzburg group of flower-sellers
1775-80
7 ⅝ in. (19.5 cm) high
Sold 4.12.78 in London for £1,400 ($2,716)

Doccia (Ginori) armorial tall flaring. beaker
c. 1750
Sold 4.12.78 in London for £1,700 ($3,298)

Elizabethan dated presentation
goblet
By Giacomo Verzelini
1584
From the Broad Street Glasshouse
6 ¼ in. (16 cm) high
Sold 3.10.78 in London for
£75,000 ($142,500)
Record auction price for glass

To date the market has been dominated by the high prices given for Venetian or German glasses, English glasses playing a minor role. The sale on 3 October 1978 of the Grenhal Verzelini goblet transformed the situation.

The discovery of this hitherto unrecorded goblet made a significant addition to the eight extant examples of glass by Giacomo Verzelini, the Venetian glassmaker who in 1575 was granted a 21-year monopoly by Queen Elizabeth I to make glass in the Italian style at his Broad Street glasshouse in London. Engraved in diamond-point and bearing English names, inscriptions and dates ranging between the years 1577 and 1590, the decoration on all these goblets is attributed to Anthony de Lysle, a Frenchman known to have worked for the Pewterers' Company at this time.

Although Richard Grenhal, the recipient of this goblet in 1584, is difficult to pin down, there seems little doubt that he was a member of the family of Greenhell or Greenhall of Blackburn, Lancashire; the heraldic devices including the Latham/Stanley crest and the Derby badge would suggest that the goblet was the gift of a member of this family, possibly related to Richard Grenhal by marriage.

Nuremberg
hausmalerei vintner's
goblet
Painted in schwarzlot
by Hermann Benckert
c. 1680
8 in. (20.5 cm) high
Sold 3.10.78 in
London for £12,000
($22,800)

Opposite far right:
Bohemian enamelled glass
jagd humpen and cover
Dated 1591
15 in. (38 cm) high
Sold 30.5.79 in London for
£13,000 ($26,000)

Opposite:
Franconian betrothal
humpen and cover
Made for Michael Menhorn
of Nuremberg in 1615
16⅛ in. (41 cm) high
Sold 30.5.79 in London for
£14,500 ($29,000)

Beilby opaque-twist goblet
c. 1770
7½ in. (19 cm) high
Sold 3.10.79 in London for £3,400 ($6,460)

Thomas Webb & Sons gem cameo oviform vase
c. 1885
8 in. (20 cm) high
Sold 3.10.78 in London for £10,000 ($19,000)

Jacobite airtwist wine-glass
Engraved with a portrait of Prince Charles
Edward, the Young Pretender, and inscribed:
Audentior Ibo
c. 1750
6½ in. (16.5 cm) high
Sold 30.5.79 in London for £2,200 ($4,400)

Baccarat butterfly and flower weight
3¼ in. (8.3 cm) diameter
Sold for £5,500 ($12,100)

Baccarat 'tri-couleur' flat bouquet
weight
3¼ in. (8.3 cm) diameter
Sold for £1,700 ($3,740)

St Louis encased double-overlay
gingham-pattern upright bouquet
weight
3⅛ in. (8 cm) diameter
Sold for £48,000 ($105,600)
World record price for any
paperweight
This hitherto unrecorded weight
exemplifies a *tour de force* in
paperweight-making which must
have involved considerable technical
difficulties, sufficient indeed to
explain why no comparable specimen
exists

St Louis white encased overlay
upright bouquet weight
3⅛ in. (8 cm) diameter
Sold for £3,200 ($7,040)

Baccarat yellow wheatflower weight
3¼ in. (8.3 cm) diameter
Sold for £2,200 ($4,840)

All sold 10.7.79 in London

Gallé mould-blown cameo
table-lamp
Signed
c. 1900
19½ in. (49.5 cm) high
Sold 27.2.79 in London for
£18,000 ($34,200)

A Boom Year for Art Nouveau and Art Deco

ALASTAIR DUNCAN

It is now difficult to distinguish between those who collect Art Nouveau and Art Deco because they appreciate it and those who collect it because it is appreciating.

The market escalated at an unprecedented rate this last season, drawing more and more collectors and investors into the field as prices spiralled upwards towards, and finally through, the $100,000 barrier. Records were set throughout the year, only to be promptly broken. The world record for Tiffany, for example, rose from $60,000 in September to $70,000 in December and, finally, to $150,000 (£75,000) in February. Prices for other artists rose accordingly. A Lalique enamel and diamond choker brought increased prices. A Larche gilt-bronze figure of Loie Fuller brought $35,000 (£17,500) in New York, twice the previous world mark. The season's most sensational prices for both Art Nouveau and Art Deco were realized in Geneva, however: a rock crystal, onyx and agate mystery clock by Cartier sold for Sw. fr. 260,000 (£80,246) in November, a seemingly insurmountable figure for an object of vertu from the 1920s. Yet in May 1979 a similar mystery clock by Van Cleef & Arpels brought Sw. fr. 650,000 (£184,659), a world record for both Art Deco and a clock. Likewise in Geneva, the Russell Bodé collection of early Gallé glass caused a sensation. The penultimate lot, an applied orchid vase, brought Sw. fr. 190,000 (£53,824), twice the previous world mark. A minute later the last lot in the sale, a marqueterie coquillage bowl, was knocked down for Sw. fr. 370,000 (£104,815), bringing to a climax a year which left the market groping to interpret these dramatic new levels in the light of past growth rates.

In general terms, the Art Nouveau market now appears to be firmly established in New York, while that of Art Deco remains in Europe. Between the two, England continues as an active part of the market, although it has yielded the bulk of its 1900-25 Decorative Arts treasures over the last ten years. Japan, too, is emerging as a major collector market, initially for pâte-de-verre and Gallé glass, but now increasingly for Tiffany lamps and French furniture. With such a broad international base the market appears sound.

Tiffany spider web
leaded glass, mosaic
and bronze table lamp
25½ in. (65 cm) high;
17½ in. (44.5 cm)
diameter of shade
Sold 17.2.79 in New
York for $150,000
(£75,000)
From the collection of
Eleanor Gluck
Record auction price
for a piece of Tiffany
glass

Gallé marqueterie-de-verre shaped coquillage cup
Engraved vertical signature to the side of the body
c. 1900
12 ³⁄₈ in. (31.5 cm) wide
Sold 20.6.79 in Geneva for Sw. fr. 370,000 (£104,815)
From the Russell Bodé Collection

L'Orchidée
Gallé glass baluster vase
Engraved signature on the lower part of the back
c. 1900
8 7/8 in. (22.5 cm) high
Sold 20.6.79 in Geneva for Sw. fr. 190,000 (£53,824)
From the Russell Bodé Collection

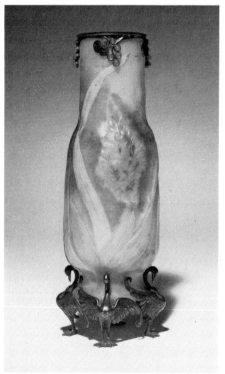

Marqueterie-de-verre glass vase
By Emile Gallé
Incised script signature: Gallé
9¼ in. (23.5 cm) high
Sold 24.5.79 in New York for
$21,000 (£10,500)

Walnut and beechwood coiffeuse
By Louis Majorelle
Sold 17.7.79 in London for £8,000
($18,080)

Gallé marqueterie-sur-verre
metal-mounted oviform vase
Sold 17.7.79 in London for £6,000
($13,560)

Opposite:
Gilt-bronze figural lamp of
Loie Fuller
Cast from a model by Raoul
Larche
c. 1900
17½ in. (44.5 cm) high
Sold 24.3.79 in New York for
$35,000 (£17,500)

Opposite far right:
Tiffany Gould peacock lamp
40½ in. (103 cm) high
Sold 1.12.78 in New York for
$70,000 (£36,269)

Tiffany wisteria and
snowball stained-glass
window
51 × 35 in. (130 × 89 cm)
Sold 17.2.79 in New York
for $48,000 (£24,000)
From the collection of
Eleanor Gluck

ORIENTAL CERAMICS AND WORKS OF ART

Pair of unglazed terracotta ladies astride galloping polo ponies
T'ang Dynasty
About 15½ in. (39.5 cm) long
Sold 9.11.78 in New York for $55,000 (£27,500)
From the collection of Mr and Mrs Otto Doering, Snr

Glazed buff pottery
figure of a standing
Bactrian camel
T'ang Dynasty
22 ¼ in. (56.5 cm)
high
Sold 11.12.78 in
London for £9,500
($18,050)
From the collection of
the late Frank W.
Pierce
Sold on behalf of the
National Art
Collections Fund

One of a pair of famille rose peach
dishes
Yung Chêng six-character marks and
of the period
Sold for $65,000 (£32,500)

Carved Ting Yao plate
Northern Sung Dynasty
Sold for $120,000 (£60,000)

All sold 9.11.78 in New York
From the collection of Mr and Mrs Otto Doering, Snr

Brilliantly painted Tz'u Chou jar and
cover
Northern Sung Dynasty
Sold for $48,000 (£24,000)

Green-glazed pottery broad oviform jar
T'ang Dynasty
10½ in. (27 cm) diameter; 10¼ in. (26 cm) high
Sold 9.7.79 in London for £17,500 ($38,500)

Chun-Yao 'bubble'
bowl
Sung Dynasty
3¾ in. (9.5 cm)
diameter
Sold 9.7.79 in London
for £23,000 ($50,600)

Ming yellow and green
square bowl
Chia Ching six-
character mark in
underglaze blue and of
the period
7½ in. (19 cm) square
Sold 9.11.78 in New
York for $68,000
(£34,000)
From the collection of
Mr and Mrs Otto
Doering, Snr

Celadon pear-shaped
bottle
Koryŏ Dynasty,
12th/13th century
11 in. (28 cm) high
Sold 9.7.79 in London
for £16,500 ($36,300)

Ying Ching wine ewer
and cover
Yüan Dynasty, first
quarter of the 14th
century
The ewer 11 in.
(28 cm) high, with
cover 13¼ in.
(33.5 cm) high
Sold 9.11.78 in New
York for $260,000
(£130,000)
From the collection of
Mr and Mrs Otto
Doering, Snr

Opposite:
Large Ming blue and
white jar
Chia Ching six-
character mark and of
the period
21½ in. (54.5 cm)
high
Sold 9.11.78 in New
York for $75,000
(£37,500)
From the collection of
Mr and Mrs Otto
Doering, Snr

White-glazed stem-cup
(*kao-tsu wan*)
Yung Lo
6 1/8 in. (15.6 cm)
diameter
Sold 11.12.78 in
London for £40,000
($76,000)

Ming blue and yellow
saucer-dish
Encircled Hung Chih
six-character mark and
of the period
10³⁄₈ in. (26.5 cm)
diameter
Sold 11.12.78 in
London for £50,000
($95,000)

Large polychrome
beaker vase
Wan Li six-character
mark in a rectangle on
the exterior of the rim
and of the period
27 in. (68.5 cm) high
Sold 11.12.78 in
London for £6,500
($12,350)

Large famille verte
saucer-dish
Encircled *chih* (made
to order) mark,
K'ang Hsi
20½ in. (52 cm)
diameter
Sold 25.6.79 in
London for £4,200
($8,820)

Pair of famille verte
figures of seated
Buddhistic lions
K'ang Hsi
10 in. (25.5 cm) high
Sold 25.6.79 in
London for £3,000
($6,300)
From the collection of
the late Hans Mettler

Export globular teapot
and shallow-domed
cover
Yung Chêng/early
Ch'ien Lung
Sold 25.6.79 in
London for £4,400
($9,240)

Pair of massive cloisonné enamel baluster vases
Late 18th/early 19th century
42 in. (106.5 cm) high
Sold 19.3.79 in London for £12,000 ($24,600)

Archaic bronze tripod
cauldron (*ting*)
Late Shang Dynasty
10¼ in. (26 cm) high;
8½ in. (21.5 cm)
diameter
Sold 9.7.79 in London
for £21,000 ($46,200)

Mottled white, pale, apple and emerald green jade flattened baluster vase
6 in. (15.2 cm) high
Sold for £4,500 ($8,550)
Sold on behalf of the Judith E. Wilson Fund of the University of Cambridge

Semi-translucent mottled emerald green, russet and greyish-white jade brush-washer
6 in. (16.8 cm) long
Sold for £3,200 ($6,080)

Both sold 14.12.78 in London

Mottled spinach green
jade boulder
18th century
8 in. (20.3 cm) high
Sold 14.12.78 in
London for £9,500
($18,050)

Large mottled dark
celadon jade boulder
17th/18th century
12 ¾ in. (32.3 cm)
high
Sold 4.4.79 in London
for £18,000 ($36,000)

Mottled greyish-
celadon jade brush pot
Ch'ien Lung
6¾ in. (17.2 cm) high
Sold 4.4.79 in London
for £17,000 ($34,000)

Mottled white, brown
and pale celadon jade
boulder
18th century
7 ⅛ in. (18.1 cm) high
Sold 11.7.79 in
London for £7,000
($15,470)

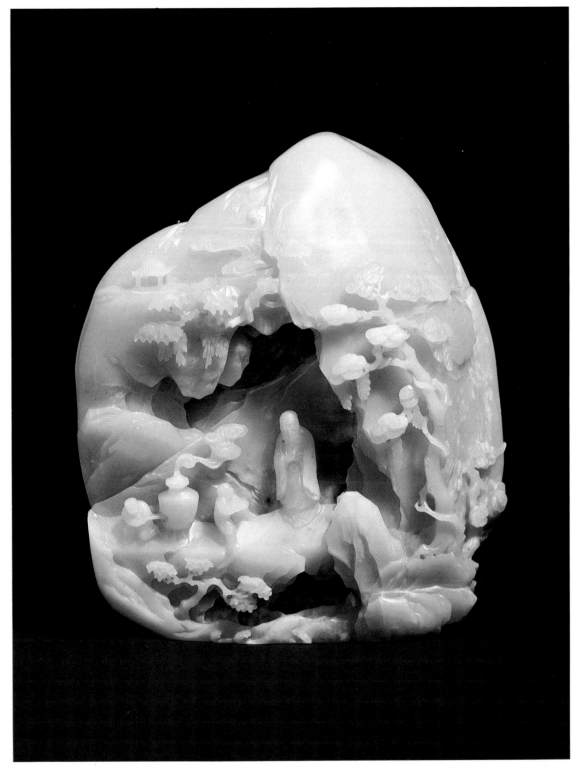

Collection of ivory
netsuke
Sold individually
6.3.79 in London for
a total of £15,490
($30,980)

Collection of wood
netsuke
Sold individually
6.3.79 in London for
a total of £14,930
($29,860)

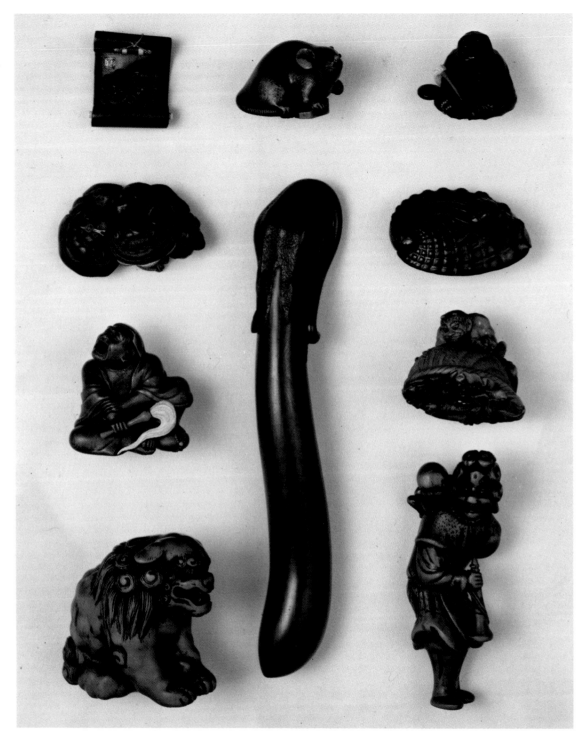

Rectangular kodansu
19th century, $13 \times 9\frac{5}{8} \times 8\frac{1}{8}$ in. ($33.1 \times 24.4 \times 20.8$ cm)
Sold for £4,500 ($8,820)

Pair of cylindrical lacquer vases
signed on the bases: Kinkendo Kaneko san within floral surrounds
Late 19th century, $14\frac{3}{8}$ in. (36.4 cm) high
Sold for £6,500 ($12,740)
From the collection of the late Gladys Marie, Dowager Duchess of Marlborough

All sold 13.12.78 in London

Rectangular kodansu
19th century
13 ¾ × 8 ¾ × 7 ⅝ in.
(35.9 × 22.2
 × 19.5 cm)
Sold for £9,000
($17,640)

Rectangular kodansu
19th century
13 ¼ × 12 ¼ × 8 ½ in.
(33.5 × 31 × 21.7 cm)
Sold for £10,000
($19,600)

Both sold 13.12.78 in
London

Group of ceremonial
lacquer wares from a
bridal set
Late 19th century
Sold individually
13.12.78 in London
for a total of £21,485
($42,110)

Pair of Imari figures of
smiling bijin
Genroku period
17⅝ in. (44.7 cm) high
Sold 27.3.79 in London for £5,500
($11,000)

Silver and lacquer three-piece
garniture
One vase signed on an oval tablet:
Masayuki
Late 19th century
The vases 11¾ in. (29.9 cm) high
Sold 27.3.79 for £4,500 ($9,000)

Left to right:
Silver and gold lacquer
vase
Late 19th century
12½ in. (31.7 cm)
high
Sold for £2,000
($4,180)

Silver and ivory
vessel and domed
cover
Late 19th century
10⅝ in. (26.9 cm)
high
Sold for £2,700
($5,643)

Silvered-metal and
lacquer vessel
and domed cover
Late 19th century
12⅛ in. (30.7 cm)
high
Sold for £2,600
($5,434)

Left to right
Gold, silver, copper
and shibuichi table
screen
Late 19th century
9⅜ in. (23.8 cm) high
Sold for £3,400
($7,106)

Ivory-mounted
lacquer table screen
Late 19th century
Each leaf 9⅝ × 5⅝ in.
(24.5 × 14.4 cm)
Sold for £1,900
($3,971)

All sold 20.6.79 in
London

Bronze rectangular
small cabinet
Signed on the front of
one drawer Otake
Norikuni above a
square gold seal
Nori, late 19th century
14 × 13⅝ × 6¾ in.
(35.7 × 34.7
× 17.1 cm)
Sold 20.6.79 in
London for £8,500
($17,765)

Pair of bronze figures
of Samurai
The bases cast with the
inscription Suzuki
Masayoshi zo
Late 19th century
49¼ in. (125 cm) high
Sold 4.5.79 in New
York for $42,000
(£21,000)

ANDO HIROSHIGE:
White Rain at Shono
From the Tokaïdo
series
Sold 4.5.79 in New
York for $13,000
(£6,500)

ANDO HIROSHIGE:
Sudden Shower at Ohashi
From the Famous
Views of Edo series
Signed Hiroshige
Sold 28.11.78 in New
York for $9,500 (£4,797)

HOKUSAI: *Roben
Waterfall at Oyama in
Sagami Province*
From the Famous
Waterfalls series
Sold 28.11.78 in New
York for $4,800
(£2,424)

Beauty in Cold Steel

WILLIAM TILLEY

For more than ten centuries the Japanese sword played an important role in its country's history, until finally prohibited by the 'haitorei' edict of Emperor Meiji in 1876.

Today a fine Japanese blade is appreciated for its superb craftsmanship, for the rich colour and finely forged texture of its steel surface and the ever-changing iridescence of the whitish tempered line along the edge — an edge which, for all its beauty, can sever a human body with a single dreadful blow. Although excellent sword-blades were produced in the 'late' period, i.e. after 1596, none can match the almost mystic refinement of those superb examples produced in late Heian and early Kamakura times, roughly mid-11th to mid-14th century. These were the great days of the Japanese sword, and although blades from this period are rare outside Japan, an important group was sold by Christie's on 5 June 1979. All were in the plain wood scabbards or shirasaya in which blades are kept when not mounted for use, and only two of the collection of fifteen were from the new sword period, i.e. after 1596.

Perhaps the finest was a tachi blade by Ichimonji Nobufusa of Bizen province (late 12th to early 13th century), one of a select group of swordsmiths summoned from all over Japan to work with the Emperor Gotoba-in soon after his accession in 1184. Gotoba himself made swords, a few of which survive, signed only with the Imperial chrysanthemum crest, and the swordsmiths who worked with him are known as 'Goban-Kaji' or Imperial Guard smiths. The blade by Nobufusa, which realized £26,000 ($54,340), was made for a slung sword to be worn on horseback; the popular 'samurai' sword, worn edge upwards in the sash, was not to appear for another two centuries. At this early period swordsmiths mined their own iron, and mountainous areas such as Hoki and Bizen, famous for iron ore, became centres of sword-making.

Other outstanding blades in the collection, dating from the 13th or 14th centuries, were by Masatsune (£15,000, $31,350), Motoshige (£11,000, $22,990), Nagamitsu (£8,200, $17,138) and Morokage (£6,000, $12,540), all of Bizen province; Sadatsuna of Hoki province (£13,000, $27,170), and Suketsuna of Sagami (£13,000, $27,170).

Only two of the blades were of recent date — a katana blade by Taikei Naotane dated 1829, and another by Yokoyama Sukesada dated 1890. Naotane (1779-1857) was the foremost pupil of Suishinshi Masahide who led the 19th-century revival of sword-making by an attempted return to ancient methods; he worked in both Bizen and Sagami styles, and his blades sometimes had carved decoration done by his pupil Yoshitane.

The blade by Yokoyama Sukesada also exemplifies the respect later swordsmiths felt for the early masters, for it is inscribed '59th in descent from Tomonari' (a famous 10th-century Bizen smith). Dated 1890, fourteen years after the wearing of swords in public was forbidden, this last blade may well have been made to order for the unknown person who formed this exceptional collection.

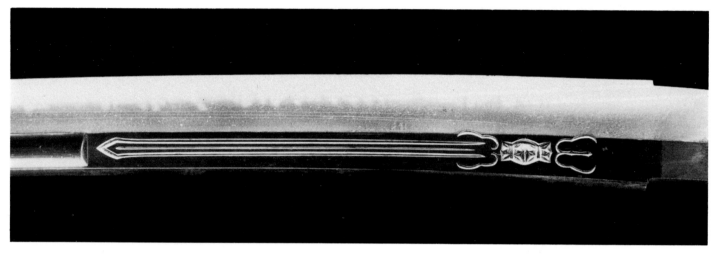

Detail of a sword-blade by Taikei Naotane
Sold 5.6.79 in London for £8,000 ($16,720)

Antique Chinese carpet
18th century
196 × 87 in. (497 × 221 cm)
Sold 24.10.78 in New York for $12,000
(£6,000)

Kashan Mochtashan prayer rug
76 × 52 in. (192 × 132 cm)
Sold 24.10.78 in New York for $10,000 (£5,000)

Antique Feraghan 'Zelli Sultan' rug
78 × 50 in. (198 × 127 cm)
Sold 12.10.78 in London for £22,000
($41,800)

Antique Beshir carpet
152 × 74 in. (387 × 188 cm)
Sold 7.6.79 in London for £5,300
($10,600)

Heriz silk rug
76 × 55 in. (193 × 140 cm)
Sold 12.10.78 in London for
£15,000 ($28,500)
From the collection of the
late Gladys Marie, Dowager
Duchess of Malborough

Tabriz carpet of Safavid design
251 × 119 in. (637 × 302 cm)
Sold 19.4.79 in London for
£11,500 ($23,000)

Persian Gambroon bowl
18th century
5½ in. (14 cm) diameter
Sold 20.4.79 in London for £1,500
($3,000)

Timurid polychrome wood chest
15th century
42 × 24 × 24 in. (107 × 61 × 61 cm)
Sold 16.10.78 in London for £6,500
($12,350)

Mamluk inlaid brass bowl
14th century
6½ in. (16.5 cm) diameter
Sold 16.10.78 in London for £750
($1,425)

Hsuan Tê gilt bronze group of Makakala
Second quarter 15th century
29 in. (74 cm) high
Sold 13.6.79 in London for £15,000 ($30,000)

Early Nepalese pata
Late 15th/early 16th century
19 ½ × 17 ½ in. (49.5 × 44.5 cm)
Sold 13.6.79 in London for £13,000 ($26,000)
From the collection of George P. Bickford

Mysore bronze Jain shrine figure of Ambika
11th/12th century
15 in. (38.5 cm) high
Sold 13.6.79 in London for £5,000 ($10,000)
From the collection of George P. Bickford

Chola bronze figure of Parvati
11th/12th century
Pudokatai style
33¼ in. (59 cm) high
Sold 13.6.79 in London for £15,000 ($30,000)
From the collection of George P. Bickford

AMIR KHUSRAW: *Qirān al Sa'Dain,* The
Conjunction of the Two Lucky Planets
Poetical account of the meeting of Sultan
Mu'izz ud-Din Kaikhubad and his father
Nasir ud-Din Bughra Khan, Sultan of Bengal
Persian manuscript, 135 leaves, 14 lines of
very fine black *nasta'liq*
One of two miniatures
Leaf $9\frac{7}{8} \times 6\frac{1}{4}$ in. (25 × 16 cm)
Sold 12.10.78 in London for £55,000
($104,500)

Kamod Ragini
Kulu, *c.* 1700-10
Leaf 8⅛ × 8⅛ in. (20.8 × 20.8 cm)
Sold 19.4.79 in London for £6,500 ($13,000)
Formerly in the George P. Bickford Collection

A seated Peri
Qazwin or Ottoman,
c. mid-16th century
Sold 19.4.79 in
London for £12,000
($24,000)
Sold on behalf of the
estate of the late
Vera Amherst Hale
Pratt

Portrait of Maharaja Jaswant Singh of Jodhpur
Jodhpur, *c.* 1645
9 3/8 × 5 1/4 in. (23.6 × 13.5 cm);
leaf 11 1/4 × 6 1/4 in. (28.5 × 16 cm)
Sold 19.4.79 in London for £3,800 ($7,600)

Equestrian portrait of Maharaja Pratap Singh of Kishangarh
hawking
Kishangarh, 1790-5
10 × 8 in. (25.6 × 20.5 cm); leaf 13 1/2 × 11 1/8 in. (34.5 × 28.4 cm)
Sold 19.4.79 in London for £4,800 ($9,600)

ETHNOGRAPHICA AND ANTIQUITIES

A Missionary in the South Seas

HERMIONE WATERFIELD

John Williams, a missionary, is the man most closely associated with the art of Rarotonga, the chief southern island of the Cook group in the Pacific. He was taken there by one of the island's kings, Makea, in 1823, having failed in an earlier attempt to find the island by himself, and was the first European to record it in detail and 'put it on the map'.

He left there a native convert from Raiatea, Papeiha, who was joined a few months later by his colleague Tiberio. These two converts unwittingly caused the destruction of nearly all the staff gods of the island. To convince the natives of their folly in worshipping these false wooden gods he and his companion burnt several and ate the bananas which they roasted in the ashes. When the natives saw there were no ill effects on the converts they proceeded to burn the idols themselves on a great scale. Some were rescued and sent back to London. Williams describes such a scene in the book he wrote after his return to Europe (*A Narrative of Missionary Enterprises in the South Sea Islands,* London, 1837): 'They walked in procession, and dropped at our feet fourteen immense idols, the smallest of which was about five yards in length. Each of these was composed of a piece of airo, or ironwood, about four inches in diameter, carved with rude imitations of the human head at one end, and with an obscene figure at the other, wrapped round with native cloth, until it became two or three yards in circumference. Near the wood were red feathers, and a string of small pieces of polished pearl shells, which were said to be the manava, or soul of the god. Some of these idols were torn to pieces before our eyes; others were reserved to decorate the rafters of the chapel we proposed to erect, and one was kept to be sent to England which is now in the Missionary Museum'. Thus the tops of the staff gods were preserved both because they were easier to transport that way and also because the missionaries regarded the phallus end as 'obscene'.

When Williams returned to Rarotonga on 6 May 1827, he was gratified to see that 'All the females wore bonnets, and were dressed in white cloth, whilst the men wore clothes and hats of native manufacture'. He 'did not intend to have remained more than three or four months at Rarotonga; but no opportunity being afforded of leaving the island, we continued there a year'.

Rarotonga head of a staff god
19 in. (48 cm) high
Sold 19.6.79 in London for £110,000
($231,000)

Easter Island wood female figure,
moai paapaa
22 ½ in. (57.5 cm) high
Sold 19.6.79 in London for £65,000
($136,500)

Fiji whale-ivory and
pearl-shell pectoral,
civa
Rewa district,
Viti Levu
9 in. (23 cm) diameter
Sold 19.6.79 in
London for £28,000
($58,800)

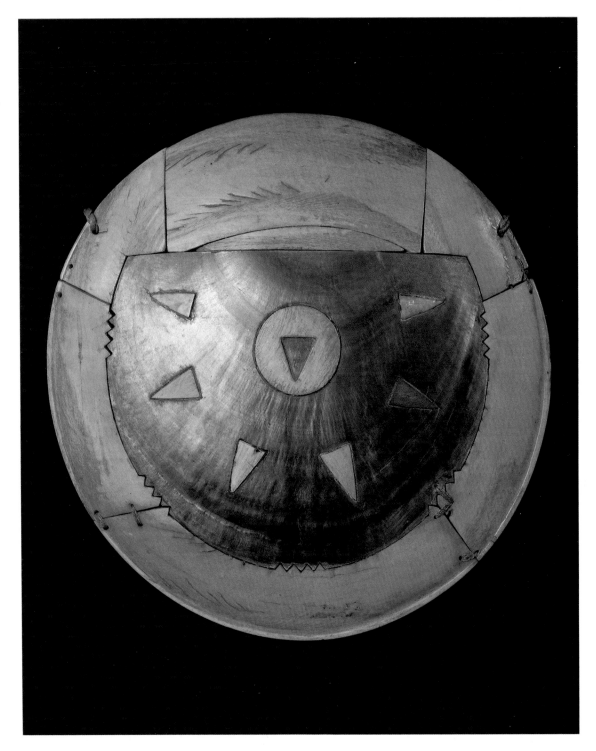

Torres Straits
turtleshell mourner's
mask
13 in. (33 cm) long
Sold 19.6.79 in
London for £40,000
($84,000)

Torres Straits wood
canoe-prow ornament
Saibai Island
13¼ in. (34 cm) wide
Sold 19.6.79 in
London for £8,000
($16,800)

New Ireland wood
friction gong
21 in. (53 cm) long
Sold 19.6.79 in
London for £6,000
($12,600)

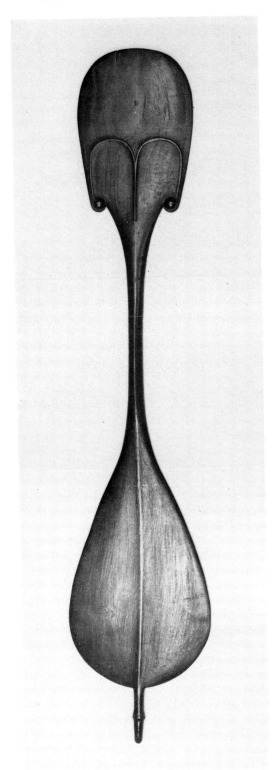

Far left:
Easter Island wood dance paddle, *rapa*
33 in. (84 cm) high
Sold 19.6.79 in London for £35,000 ($73,500)
From the Hooper Collection

Easter Island standing male figure, *moai tangata*
10½ in. (26.5 cm) high
Sold 19.6.79 in London for £15,000 ($31,500)
From the Hooper Collection

New Guinea wood crest
Second half of the 19th century
18½ in. (47 cm) long
Sold 24.10.78 in London for £9,000 ($18,000)

New Ireland wood
figure, *totok*
Medina area of
northern New Ireland
68 in. (172 cm) high
Sold 20.3.79 in
London for £9,000
($18,000)
From the collection of
the late Josef Mueller

Maori wood house post, *pou tokomanawa*
c. 1820-40
50 ½ in. (129 cm) high
Sold 24.10.78 in London for
£50,000 ($100,000)
From the collection of
J. L. H. Williams, Esq.

Opposite:
Upper part of an Egyptian
light brown quartzite figure
of Senbef
Dynasty XXVI, 664-610 BC
14 in. (35.6 cm) high
Sold 14.6.79 in New York
for $95,000 (£45,454)
Sold on behalf of the
Lord's New Church which is
Nova Hierosolyma, Bryn
Athyn, Pennsylvania
When cleaned, this statue
has been revealed carved in
nearly white, not yellow,
quartzite.

Egyptian bronze statue of a king on one knee presenting an offering table
Late Dynasty XX-Dynasty XXI
On wood stand
10⅛ in.
(25.7 cm) high
Sold 21.11.78 in London for £50,000 ($100,000)

Cycladic marble head
c. 2500 BC
7 ½ in. (19 cm) high
Sold 31.5.79 in
London for £20,000
($40,000)

Egyptian hollow-cast
bronze statue of a
seated cat
Dynasty XXVI
9 in. (23 cm) high
Sold 31.5.79 in
London for £8,000
($16,000)

Egyptian black granite statue of a royal
priestess of the Goddess Mut
Dynasty XIX
c. Ramses II, 1304-1237 BC
37 in. (94 cm) high
Sold 14.6.79 in New York for $220,000
(£105,263)
Sold on behalf of the Lord's New church
which is Nova Hierosolyma, Bryn
Athyn, Pennsylvania
World record price for a New Kingdom
sculpture

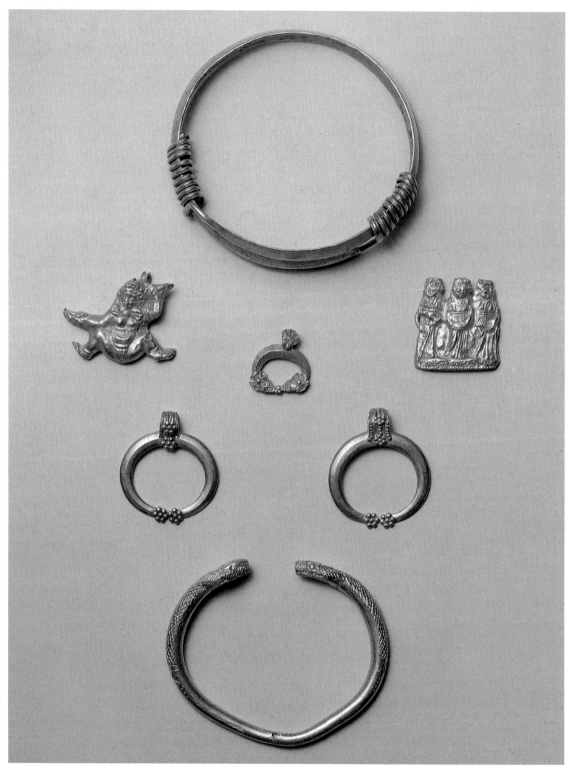

Selection from a sale of
ancient Egyptian gold
jewellery
The pieces illustrated
sold 1.6.79 in London
for a total of £9,550
($19,100)

Greek marble head of
a woman from a grave
stele
Attica, *c.* 340-330 BC
11 ¾ in. (30 cm) high
Sold 5.5.79 in Geneva
for Sw. fr. 90,000
(£25,568)

Sassanian solid-cast bronze statue of a horse
3rd-6th century AD
5 ¾ in. (14.6 cm) high; 6 ¾ in. (17.5 cm) long
Sold 31.5.79 in London for £20,000 ($40,000)

ARMS AND ARMOUR, AND MODERN SPORTING GUNS

Modern Sporting Guns and Vintage Firearms

CHRISTOPHER BRUNKER

A distinctive feature of well-made sporting guns is their long working life, during which they retain a high value in relation to their initial cost. Their perfected design and sound construction mean infrequent need for replacement, and the typical gun outlasts several owners. Gunmakers have long accepted this penalty of their skills and have eased its effect by dealing in second-hand guns. What they did not foresee was Value Added Tax, which is imposed on the full resale value of a gun each time it passes through their hands. In theory, the tax is paid by the consumer, but to remain competitive the legitimate trade has been forced to absorb much VAT in its margin. The recent increase in VAT enlarged the burden and one doubts whether the trade can sustain it without loss. The antique trade has a special scheme to reduce the tax element in its selling price. The gun trade, though smaller and perhaps less popular, deserves equal consideration, for all the tax characteristics of antiques apply to sporting guns. Further, the retailing of second-hand guns is a vital prop to the craft side of the trade. In this context, we are already living largely on inherited capital, for most of the British guns now in circulation were made by firms that no longer exist. VAT is under review, but unless the principle that nothing should be taxed twice on its full value is applied here soon, the art of gunmaking in Britain could be lost. If this occurs, the term 'value added' would acquire an ironic ring.

Over-and-under sidelock ejector 12-bore (2½ in.) double-barrelled gun By Boss, built in 1938 Sold 29.11.78 in London for £9,000 ($17,550)

426

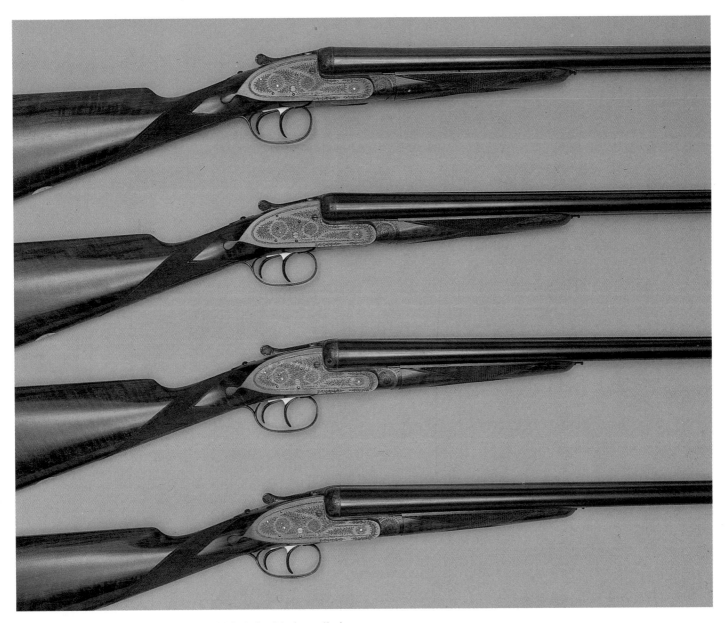

Set of four sidelock ejector 12-bore (2 ¾ in.) double-barrelled guns
By J. Purdey, completed in 1976 and unused
Sold 20.6.79 in London for £34,000 ($72,760)

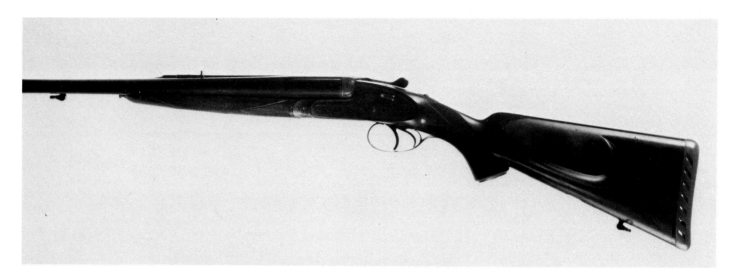

Above:
'Royal' sidelock ejector
.500/.465 double-
barrelled rifle
By Holland & Holland,
built in 1925
Sold 18.10.78 for £7,500
($15,000)

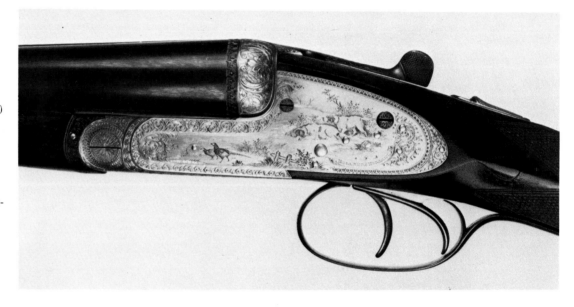

'Royal' sidelock ejector
12-bore (2 ¾ in.) double-
barrelled gun
By Holland & Holland,
built in 1896
Sold 20.6.79 for £3,600
($7,704)

Hammer 4-bore double-
barrelled punt-gun
By T. Bland, built in
1910
Sold 18.10.78 for £1,800
($3,600)

All sold in London

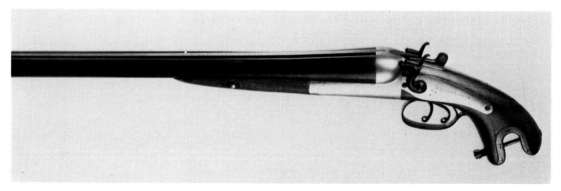

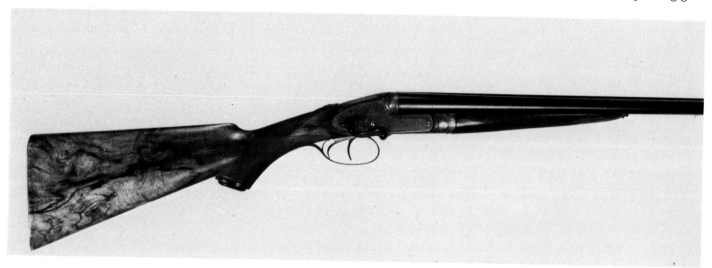

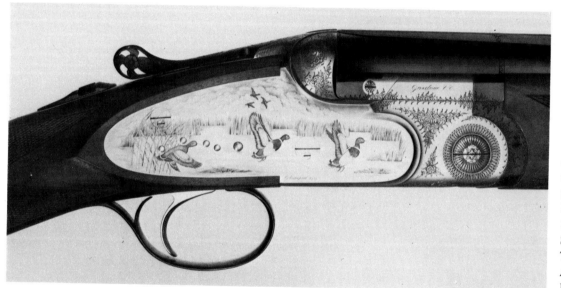

Above:
Sidelock ejector 28-bore
(2¾ in.) double-barrelled
gun, with sidelever action
By S. Grant, built in 1895
Sold 20.6.79 for £3,000
($6,420)

'Jubilee' under-and-over
sidelock ejector 12-bore
(2¾ in.) double-barrelled
gun
By P. Beretta, built in
1977
Sold 29.11.78 on behalf of
The Wildfowlers'
Association of Great
Britain and Ireland for
£4,000 ($7,800)

Pair of sidelock ejector
12-bore (2½ in.) double-
barrelled guns
By J. Dickson, built in
1906
Sold 14.3.79 for £6,000
($12,360)

All sold in London

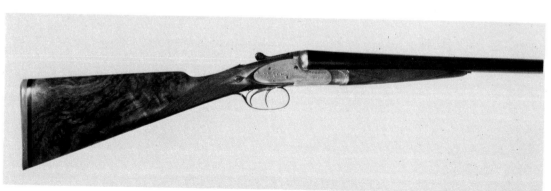

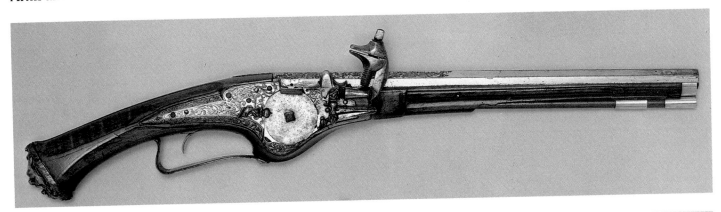

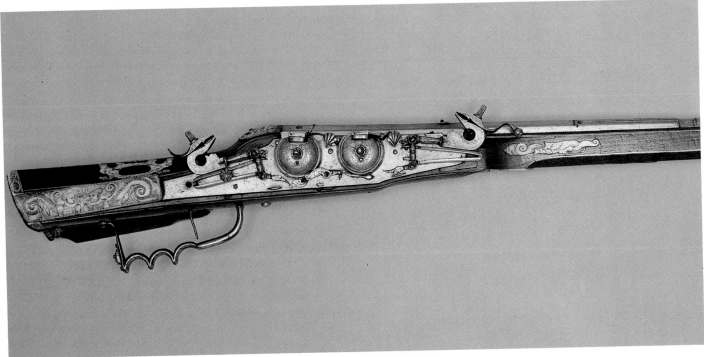

Top:
Swiss wheel-lock holster pistol
By Felix Werder of Zürich
c. 1640
20 ¼ in. (51.5 cm)
Sold 20.6.79 in London for £10,000 ($21,000)

Saxon superimposed load wheel-lock rifle
By Zacharias Herold of Dresden
Dated 1593
33 ½ in. (85 cm) barrel
Sold 1.11.78 in London for £9,500 ($19,000)

Pair of Dutch ivory-stocked flintlock holster pistols
By Johan Louroux
Maastricht, *c.* 1670/80
19 ¾ in. (50 cm)
Sold 1.11.78 in London for £36,000 ($72,000)

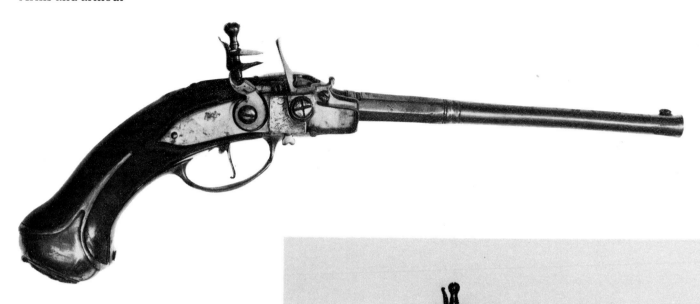

German breech-loading flintlock
magazine pistol with Lorenzoni actions
First quarter of the 18th century
16½ in. (42 cm)
Sold 1.11.78 in London for £7,000
($14,000)

Flintlock four-barrel revolver
Signed inside the lock: Mathi
Bramhofer Augspurg
c. 1750
12 in. (30.5 cm)
Sold 20.6.79 in London for £7,200
($15,120)

German wheel-lock pistol
Maker's mark an open hand flanked by
initials P D
Late 16th century
17 in. (43 cm)
Sold 20.12.78 in London for £7,500
($15,000)

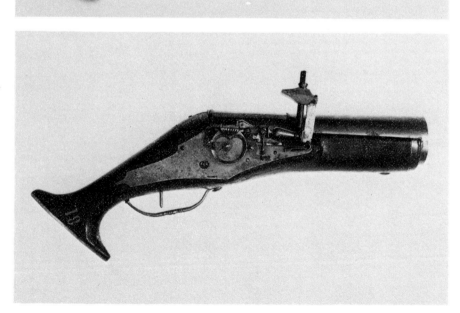

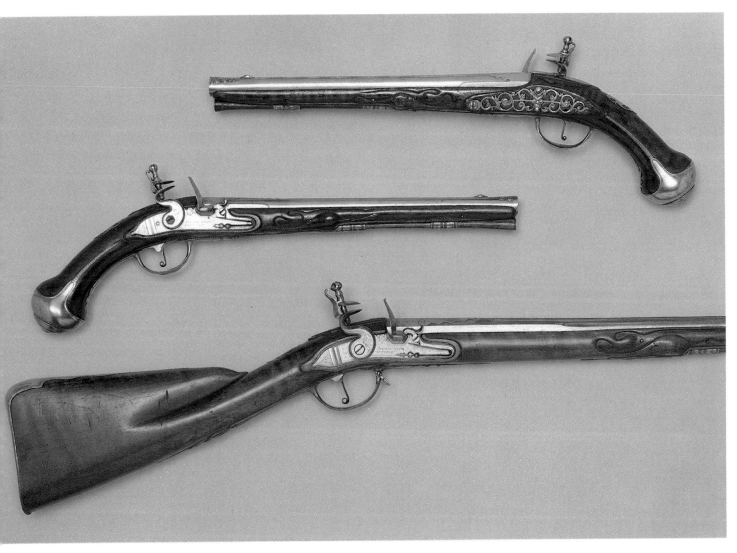

Dutch flintlock sporting garniture
By Jan van Wyck à Utrecht
Early 18th century
The gun with 45 in. (114.5 cm) barrel; the pistols 20 in. (51 cm)
Sold 20.6.79 in London for £15,000 ($31,500)

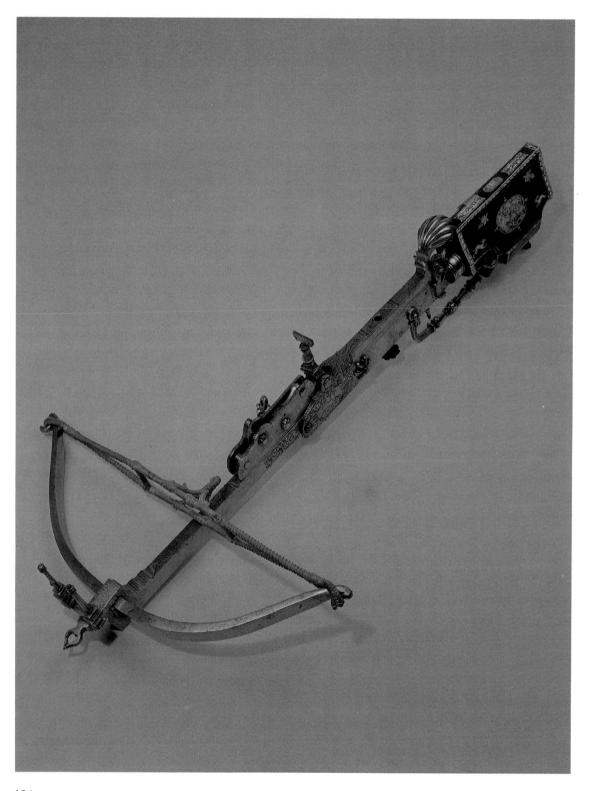

German stone-bow
Early 17th century
27½ in. (70 cm)
Sold 20.12.78 in
London for £26,000
($49,400)

North Italian half-
armour
Probably made for a
Prince of Savoy
Early 17th century
Sold 20.6.79 in
London for £23,000
($48,300)

435

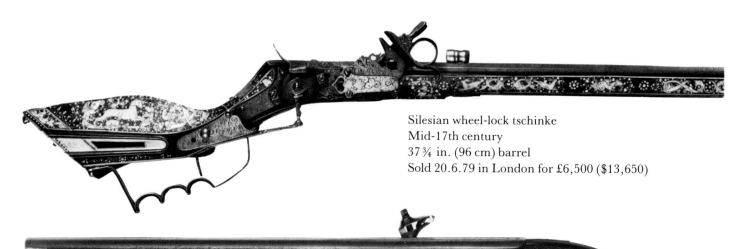

Silesian wheel-lock tschinke
Mid-17th century
37¾ in. (96 cm) barrel
Sold 20.6.79 in London for £6,500 ($13,650)

Above:
Dutch long wheel-lock holster pistol
Probably by Jan Kitzen
Maastricht, *c.* 1650
27¼ in. (69 cm)
Sold 1.11.78 in London for £4,500 ($9,000)

French 16-bore DB percussion sporting gun
Signed: Gastinne Renette, Arquebusier de
S.M. l´Empereur à Paris
c. 1860
26 in. (66 cm) barrels
Sold 1.11.78 in London for £9,000 ($18,000)

Two Scottish swords with signed basket hilts
By John Simpson the Younger of Glasgow
First half of the 18th century
Left: Sold for £1,500 ($3,150)
Right: Sold for £1,250 ($2,625)
Both sold 7.6.79 in Glasgow
From the Red Hackle Whisky Collection

SALES IN ROME AND THE NETHERLANDS

ANDREAS 'ANDRIES' SCHELFHOUT:
Figures Skating on a Frozen Lake
Indistinctly signed, on panel
$16\frac{3}{8} \times 21\frac{5}{8}$ in. (41.5 × 55 cm)
Sold 30.10.78 for D. fl. 55,000
(£14,102)

HENRIETTE 'H. RONNER' KNIP:
A Proud Mother
Signed
$21\frac{5}{8} \times 28\frac{1}{2}$ in. (55 × 72.5 cm)
Sold 30.10.78 for D. fl. 32,000
(£8,205)

Circular chamber candlestick
By Jacob van der Hoop
Amsterdam, 1737
Sold 4.4.79 for D. fl. 17,000 (£4,071)

Delft pottery tile
Late 16th century
Sold 3.4.79 for
D. fl. 8,500 (£2,040)
World record auction
price for a tile

Siegburg white
stoneware Schnelle
Dated 1591
Sold 4.4.79 for
D. fl. 13,000
(£3,113)

Pair of Dutch Delft butter dishes and cover formed as sitting
hens
By Hendrik van Middeldijk, in 't' Hart
Mid-18th century
Sold 31.10.78 for D. fl. 24,000 (£6,153)
From the collection of the late Benjamin Katz

Four Louis XV candlesticks
By Dirk Blom
Amsterdam, 1758
Sold 1.11.78 for D. fl. 25,000
(£6,402)

Rare windmill beaker
Delft 1661, perhaps by Barend Fast
Sold 1.11.78 for D. fl. 32,000 (£8,194)

Kraakporselein dish
Wan Li
Sold 1.11.78 for D. fl. 8,000 (£2,048)

Pair of slender baluster-formed eggshell
porcelain Rozenburg vases
Decorated by T. Schelling
Marked: Rozenburg Den Haag
Dated 1902
14½ in. (37 cm) high
Sold 1.11.78 for D.fl. 15,000 (£3,841)

Selection from a George III silver service
By Paul Storr
London, 1812
Sold 24.5.79 for L. 9,000,000 (£6,000)

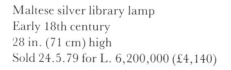

Maltese silver library lamp
Early 18th century
28 in. (71 cm) high
Sold 24.5.79 for L. 6,200,000 (£4,140)

GIOVANNI BOLDINI:
Lezione di Musica
Signed, on board
5¾ × 9 in. (14.5 × 23 cm)
Sold 18.5.79 for
L. 17,000,000
(£11,340)

JAN WILDENS: *Landscape
with Falconers and a Ferry*
55 × 80 in. (140 × 205 cm)
Sold 18.5.79 for
L. 20,000,000
(£13,340)

Roman centre table in neoclassical taste
c. 1790
34¼ in. (87 cm) high; 39⅜ in.
(100 cm) wide
Sold 2.11.78 for L. 11,000,000 (£7,340)

South Italian chest of drawers
Early 18th century
40½ in. (103 cm) high; 60 in.
(155 cm) wide
Sold 3.11.78 for L. 12,500,000 (£8,340)

Both sold by order of the Executors of
Donna Maria Sofia dei Principi
Giustiniani-Bandini, Contessa Gravina
dei Principi di Ramacca, Countess of
Newburgh

From 2 to 6 November 1978, following
the death of Donna Maria Sofia
dei Principi Giustiniani-Bandini,
Contessa Gravina dei Principi di
Ramacca and Countess of Newburgh,
Christie's sold the contents of the
Giustiniani-Bandini villa in Rome.
Just across the Tiber from the Piazza
del Popolo, this house, once the hub of
Roman society, had been closed for
twenty years and thus the sale was a
day of discovery for many. When the
dust of years had been swept away,
over 1,800 lots were revealed to an
avid public, and the total sold,
769,534,000 lire (£513,430), exceeded
that of any dispersal in Rome since
the war.

LORENZO DI BICCI: *The Madonna Enthroned with Saints*
On panel, arched
$34\,^5/_8 \times 20\,^1/_2$ in. (88 × 52 cm)
Sold 18.5.79 for L. 19,000,000 (£12,670)

AMBROGIO DA FOSSANO (BERGOGNONE): *The Betrothal of the Virgin*
On panel
$74 \times 58\,^5/_8$ in. (187 × 149 cm)
Sold 7.12.78 for L. 22,000,000 (£14,670)

Large Palermo SPQP albarello
14½ in. (36 cm) high
Sold 10.5.79 for L. 5,200,000 (£3,470)

German high-relief
Probably Ulm, late 15th century
33½ in. (85 cm) high; 25½ in.
(65 cm) wide
Sold 26.4.79 for L. 7,500,000 (£5,000)

CHRISTIE'S EAST

_____

Christie's East

RAY PERMAN

The success of Christie's Park Avenue brought demand earlier this year for a comprehensive service similar to that at Christie's South Kensington in London and led to the opening of Christie's East in March. To do this we acquired a sixth-storey garage on East 67th Street.

Since April we have had at least 30 sales of diverse interest: 19th- and 20th-century photographs, trophy mounts of North American animals, 20th-century designer and Victorian clothes, antique and modern jewellery, carousel horses and African masks. Our 'general' sales have become a feature of Manhattan's life, including works of art of all kinds: furniture, silver, rugs, porcelain, glass, orientalia, pictures and objets d'art of every sort from ship's figureheads to Tiffany glass.

Our speciality sales of 19th- and 20th-century photographs and 'Important 20th-Century Designer Clothes' attracted tremendous public interest. Both sales produced new world records and were attended by large crowds and television networks.

The photography sale on 4 May included some rare 19th-century prints and daguerreotypes, but the fine 20th-century material, with works by Andre Kertesz, Ansel Adams and Edward Steichen, produced the most interest. Edward Weston's magnificent study 'Shell' sold for a record price of $9,500 (£4,750). The sale proved to be our most successful so far, with a total of $343,530 (£171,765).

The sale of designer clothes on 10 May created great excitement as it was the first of its kind in America. A fashion show of a selection of clothes to be sold was held before the sale, which included such names as Schiaparelli, Worth, Balenciaga and Chanel. However, the greatest interest was reserved for a fine collection of dresses by the Italian master Mariano Fortuny. One of these sold for $3,500 (£1,750) to a New York collector. A dress and jacket made the same amount and was bought by Cathy Hardwicke, a New York designer, who later donated it to the Metropolitan Museum of Art.

The results of such sales show that Christie's East is now firmly established and looks forward to an even more active season.

The Christie's East building on 67th Street,
New York City, June 1979
A former six-storey garage converted into two
floors of salerooms and four for warehousing

WILLIAM RICARBY
MILLER: *The Bay of
New York from the
Heights of Hoboken*
Signed, inscribed
N.Y.C. and dated
1860, inscribed on a
label on the reverse
25 × 37 in.
(63.5 × 94 cm)
Sold 25.4.79 for
$17,000 (£8,500)
World record auction
price for a work by this
artist

The First Japanese
Diplomatic Mission to
the United States
By Mathew Brady
(1823-96)
Fourteen highly
important imperial
prints on plain salted
paper of the members
of the Japanese
delegation which
arrived in the United
States in May 1860,
terminating over 200
years of international
isolation instituted
early in the 17th
century by Tokugawa
Ieyasu
Sold 7.11.78 for
$13,000 (£6,500) at
Christie's Park
Avenue, prior to the
opening of Christie's
East, where specialized
sales of photographica
are now held.

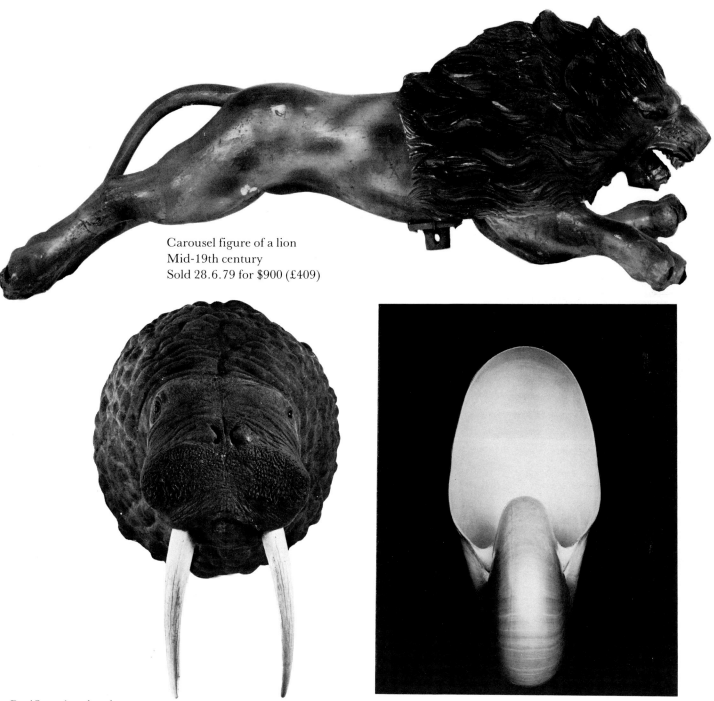

Carousel figure of a lion
Mid-19th century
Sold 28.6.79 for $900 (£409)

Pacific walrus head
Sold 20.6.79 for $2,200 (£1,000)
From the A. C. Gilbert Collection of North American
trophy mounts
Sold for the benefit of Yale's Peabody Museum

Shell
By Edward Weston
Sold 4.5.79 for $9,500 (£4,750)
World record auction price for a single 20th-century print

451

The fashion show
preceding the sale of
20th-century designer
clothes 10.5.79 at
Christie's East
The dress on the
right was sold for
$3,500 (£1,750), a
world record auction
price for the designer
(Fortuny)

THE CHANEL SALE

The Chanel Sale

SUSAN MAYOR

On Saturday night, 2 December 1978, Christie's auctioned 'Coco' Chanel's personal wardrobe and casket of costume jewellery, eight years after her death at the remarkable age of 87. As Madge Garland said in her foreword to the catalogue: 'More than any other couturier of her time, Chanel reflected in her work the immense changes which came over the lives of all Western women after the First World War'. Or, as Picasso remarked, Chanel had invented 'la pauvreté de luxe'. It was an evening which made saleroom history, arousing extraordinary international interest. Twelve television networks covered the sale, and 1,500 enthusiasts and scores of determined buyers thronged the Great Rooms. Many of those attending were dressed appropriately — not a few in the little black dresses and beautiful jewellery Chanel recommended 'for little evenings anywhere in the World'. The saleroom was decorated entirely with white flowers, just as Chanel liked for the presentation of her own collections.

The sale started a little late — something quite unheard-of for important sales — as it took time to steer everyone to their seats and clear the way for the models. All the models were carefully chosen to look and move just as Mademoiselle would have approved. One in fact had even modelled one of Chanel's own collections.

First came the jewellery. It was Chanel who first made costume jewellery fashionable. She designed it to be worn blatantly on tweeds during the day. These were items she had often worn herself and used in shows. Lot 5 — her lucky number — was her favourite piece, a fascinating filigree brooch set with large plaques of emerald green paste and smaller simulated rubies and diamonds. This fetched £1,000 ($2,000). There was a gasp as lot 8 fetched the amazing price of £1,600 ($3,200): a brooch set with a large simulated emerald, with three simulated baroque pearls suspended below. There followed a number of Chanel's famous simulated pearl necklaces. Dior said of her: 'With a black sweater and ten rows of pearls Chanel revolutionized fashion'.

In a collection such as this one might expect designs and sketches as well as finished articles. With Chanel this was impossible. She worked directly on the materials. Sometimes her inspiration was so impetuous that she was known to break up pieces of her famous 'real' jewellery, when she did not have suitable pieces of paste to hand. The same thing happened when she designed clothes: once she even chopped up her bedroom curtains when inspired during the night.

Then came the dresses, each with a specially made label sewn in by hand by Madame Grumbach, reading 'Chanel vente chez Christie's 2 décembre 1978'. Museums entered the sale to compete with the private buyers. The first lot, the suit of beige tweed bound with pink braid she wore at her last three collections, made £2,400 ($4,800) and was bought by Oslo

454

Black sleeveless side-
buttoning dress with
three-quarter length
coat with belt
With Chanel label
Chanel made this for
herself, and wore it
with the hat, in
Switzerland and Italy,
including a film
première of Visconti's
Sold 2.12.78 in
London for £1,200
($2,400)
Hat sold for £100
($200)
Both purchased by the
Victoria and Albert
Museum

Short evening dress of
black pleated silk
chiffon with bootlace
straps and gauze jacket
Winter 1960
Sold 2.12.78 in
London for £1,500
($3,000)

Mlle Chanel's working
overall of white piqué
Sold 2.12.78 in
London for £380
($760)
Purchased by the
Museum of Costume,
Bath

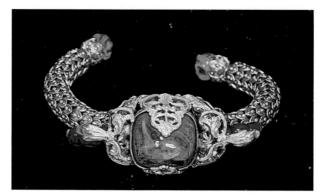

Oval filigree brooch containing four central square simulated emeralds flanked by simulated rubies and set with paste
This was Chanel's favourite piece
Sold 2.12.78 in London for £1,000 ($2,000)

Tubular bangle of gilt metal scales set with artificial pearls and paste
The last of Chanel's jewellery designs, shortly before her death, and never put into production
Sold 2.12.78 in London for £950 ($1,900)

Museum. The Victoria and Albert Museum paid £1,200 ($2,400) for a black sleeveless dress with matching coat. Castle Howard Museum acquired a suit of navy blue wool for £900 ($1,800) as well as a pair of Chanel's white piqué working overalls for £600 ($1,200). The Smithsonian Institution paid £1,000 ($2,000) for a suit of beige wool. A private buyer paid £1,500 ($3,000) for the beautiful evening dress of black pleated chiffon (winter 1960). Another private buyer paid £1,800 ($3,600) for a suit of brown printed velvet; the Beatles admired this velvet and asked Chanel where she got it. Another buyer paid £1,700 ($3,400) for a white silk three-quarter length coat and dress embroidered all over with sequins, while the last dress Chanel made for herself, a white silk chiffon dress, realized £1,500 ($3,000). It was the only long dress she wore in her later years; she wore it the day it was made, at a gala she attended with Jacques Chazot in 1970.

Next came the accessories, also fetching high prices. The Victoria and Albert Museum bought a hat of black silk stockinette with a wide brim and small bow for £100 ($200). A pair of sling-back shoes of black and white kid by Massaro, 2 Rue de la Paix, were acquired by Northampton Museum for £25 ($50). These were designed and worn by Chanel, and resemble the shoes she first produced in the 1920s and then re-launched in the 1950s. A silk scarf printed in brown with squares and linked Cs made £190 ($380), and a plain silk scarf stamped Chanel £70 ($140). The one survival from the Thirties, lot 103 — a bodice embroidered with paillettes which Chanel went on wearing after the war — made £600 ($1,200).

The whole collection was assembled by Madame Lilian Grumbach, Chanel's closest colleague during the last fourteen years of her life. It fetched £40,090 ($80,180). Saturday 2 December was indeed a fitting tribute to Coco, La Grande Couturière, and a shared triumph for Christie's King Street and Christie's South Kensington.

CHRISTIE'S
SOUTH KENSINGTON

Christie's South Kensington

WILLIAM F. BROOKS

'We Never Close.' The following pages will illustrate some of the reasons why.

It is not always appreciated that the South Kensington season extends from 1 January to 31 December with an average of fifteen sales per week, comprising some 4,000 lots. Christie's South Kensington is never afraid to pioneer new fields of interest, and among the 600 or so sales held last season were the Phyllis Neilson-Terry Collection of costume jewellery and theatrical memorabilia, the William Bishop Collection of writing implements and the Arnold & Walker Collection of tools of the carpenter and other craftsmen. A magnificent sale of natural history and sporting trophies produced a plea from the local constabulary requesting us 'to notify them in good time in future, before attempting further movement of elephant and gorilla through the streets of the Metropolis'. Traffic was in fact brought to a halt in West London, between Christie's South Kensington and the television studios at Shepherds Bush where some of the specimens were taken to be filmed.

In addition, we held sales last season at places as diverse as Wateringbury Place, Kent; South End House, Twickenham; Swithland Hall, Loughborough, Leicestershire; Serlby Hall, Doncaster; The Grange, Delamere, Cheshire; and Newbrough Lodge, Northumberland. Our programme of 'Probes' (one or two-day visits by our specialists to provincial centres throughout the United Kingdom) has taken our team over a twelve-month period to Winchester, Kendal, Preston, the Isle of Man, Port Sunlight, Llandudno, Durham, Harrogate, Oswestry, Chester, Weston-super-Mare, Wells, Broadstairs, Folkestone, Sheffield, Buxton, Streatley, Southport, Preston, Inverness, Elgin, Aberdeen, Chichester, Wilton House and Beaconsfield. Each has produced an enormous response with up to 1,000 people a day seeking free advice, thus bearing out the words of our advertisement, 'You don't have to go to London to go to Christie's', a claim already fulfilled by the tremendous support and encouragement from our colleagues in the regional offices, who are now reinforced by Christie's & Edmiston's, Glasgow.

The considerable and successful interchange between Christie's two London salerooms continues and last season Christie's South Kensington alone transferred well in excess of £500,000 ($1,000,000) worth of works of art to Christie's King Street, for inclusion in internationally important sales.

Our policy of a quick turn around and payment within a four-week cycle is maintained as our own success formula, contributing in no small way to the increase in turnover from £1,000,000 ($2,000,000) in 1975 to £12,000,000 ($24,000,000) in 1979. In whatever terms success or progress may be measured, however, neither could be achieved without the tremendous enthusiasm of all the staff at South Kensington, even through the traumas of recent computerization.

Old Sheffield plated
soup tureen and pair of
matching sauce
tureens
15¾ and 7¾ in.
(40 and 19.2 cm) high
Sold 6.10.78 for
£1,400 ($2,660)

Pair of Victorian silver candelabra
H.E. Ltd., Sheffield 1896
17 in. (43.2 cm) high
Sold 6.4.79 for £1,700 ($3,536)

Silver vesta case
By Samson Morden, 1887
Enamelled in monochrome with
Topsy Sinden in *Ondine*
Sold 5.3.79 for £105 ($210)

Victorian silver wine-jug
London 1850
14½ in. (36.2 cm) high
Sold 6.4.79 for £1,000 ($2,080)

Victorian ear-trumpet
with ivory ear-piece
and silver trumpet
Hawkesworth, Eyre &
Co., Sheffield 1845
16¼ in. (41.3 cm)
extended
Sold 2.4.79 for £520
($1,040)

459

WILLIAM HENRY MANDERS: *On the Llugwy: Old Bridge above the Swallow Falls, Bettws-Y-Coed, North Wales*
Signed and dated 94
20 × 30 in. (50.8 × 76.2 cm)
Sold 6.12.78 for £1,800
($3,492)

FREDERICK DANIEL HARDY: *Counting the Dowry*
Signed and dated 1879
18 × 23 ½ in.
(45.2 × 59.7 cm)
Sold 30.5.79 for £1,000
($2,040)

WILLIAM EDWARD
WEBB: *French Fishing
Boats off St Ives*
Signed and dated 1891
16 × 20 in.
(40.7 × 50.8 cm)
Sold 13.6.79 for £460
($961)

Studio of WALT DISNEY:
Mickey Mouse
Inscribed and dedicated
on mount
Acetate on watercolour
background
10 × 36¾ in.
(25.4 × 93.4 cm)
Sold 30.4.79 for
£300 ($600)

BASIL NIGHTINGALE: *'To be sold without reserve, owner going to the Front'*
Signed, inscribed and dated 1917
Charcoal and watercolour heightened with white, on buff paper
14½ in. × 21½ in. (37 × 54.6 cm)
Sold 13.6.79 for £180 ($378)

461

One from a fine set of twelve
19th-century mahogany
dining-chairs in the manner of
Robert Manwaring, including
two armchairs
Sold 4.4.79 for £5,500
($11,000)

One of a pair of buffalo
horn armchairs
Bearing the label of W.
Friedrich, San Antonio, Texas
Sold 20.6.79 for £1,900
($3,990)

Pair of late 19th-century
bronze figures
Signed: Moreau
23 in. (58.4 cm) high
Sold 17.1.79 for £1,050
($1,995)

George III papier-mâché tray gilt with
chinoiseries
30½ in. (77.5 cm)
Sold 16.5.79 for £400 ($816)

Opposite far left:
American 'Wells Fargo'
walnut desk
Signed: Wooton Desk Co.
42½ in. (108 cm)
Sold 21.2.79 for £3,000
($6,000)

Opposite left:
Mahogany and marquetry
longcase clock
The painted dial signed:
J. Stansfield, Manchester
Mid-19th century
99 in. (251.4 cm) high
Sold 20.12.78 for £1,050
($1,995)

Victorian walnut and
marquetry breakfast-table
60 in. (152.4 cm) diameter
Sold 18.4.79 for £2,600
($5,200)

Fine Royal Worcester coffee-
service by various artists and with
enamelled spoons
Sold 5.4.79 for £1,400 ($2,800)

Staffordshire figure of Wellington
13 in. (33 cm) high
Sold 9.4.79 for £200 ($420)

Meissen centre piece
22 in. (55.9 cm) high
Sold 14.6.79 for £900 ($1,881)

Pair of 18th-century opaque-twist
wine-glasses engraved with fruiting vines
Sold 3.4.79 for £120 ($250)

Fine 19th-century
Japanese silver, enamel
and Shibayama
incense-burner
7 in. (17.8 cm) high
Sold 29.8.78 for £1,350
($2,565)

Far right:
Unusual famille rose and
tou-ts'ai vase
Tao Kuang
16 in. (40.7 cm) high
Sold 26.3.79 for £450
($900)

Large 19th-century
Ao-Kutani jar
18 in. (45.3 cm) high
Sold 23.4.79 for £600
($1,200)

Japanese bronze falcon
15 in. (38 cm) high
Sold 14.6.79 for £580
($1,212)

Dunhill gold combination cigarette-case
4 ¾ in. (12 cm)
Sold 26.6.79 for £650 ($1,365)

Gold square-linked
panel bracelet
Signed: C. Giuliano
Sold 12.6.79 for
£1,500 ($3,090)

Rose diamond and
gem butterfly brooch
Sold 27.3.79 for £300
($600)

Victorian diamond
pendant with
detachable brooch
mount
Sold 30.1.79 for
£1,500 ($3,000)

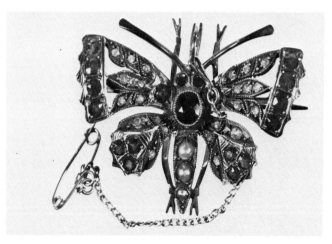

WILLIAM CAMDEN: *Britannia*
Gibson's edition, folio 1695,
50 engraved maps
Sold 20.10.78 for £900
($1,800)

Lion, full animal mount
Sold 24.3.79 for £750 ($1,500)

One of a set of six postcards
by Louis Wain
Issued by Raphael
Tuck & Sons
Sold 22.6.79 for £95 ($200)

Cinq Chevaux
Lalique motoring mascot
Sold 21.6.79 for £1,000 ($2,100)

Isambard Kingdom Brunel standing before the launching chains of *The Great Eastern*
By Robert Howlett
Albumen print, 1857 or 1858
11½ in. × 9 in. (29.2 × 22.8 cm)
Sold 15.3.79 for £7,500 ($15,225)
Record auction price for a British paper photograph

Opposite, top:
Lindisfarne
By Roger Fenton
Salt print, mid-1850s
12 × 14¾ in.
(30.5 × 37.5 cm)
Sold 28.6.79 together with another study, probably also by Fenton, for £7,500 ($15,750)

The Great Eastern

The Great Eastern was to be the supreme triumph of Isambard Kingdom Brunel (1806-59). The construction of such mammoth ocean-going steamships elevated Brunel into the realms of the engineering immortals; in 1838 his *Great Western* became the first steamship to operate a regular crossing between Britain and America. Seven years later this was surpassed by the still larger *Great Britain*. Brunel's ultimate achievement, however, was the launching of *The Great Eastern*, built to carry more than 3,000 passengers and 400 crew, in January 1858. The *Illustrated Times* commissioned Joseph Cundall, a founder member of The Calotype Club, and Robert Howlett to photograph the building and launching. Engravings based on their photographs appeared in a special 'Leviathan Number' on 16 January 1858. The text referred to '. . . photographs by Mr. Robert Howlett, one of the most skilful photographers of the day . . . and which said studies are amongst the most attractive features of the printsellers' shop windows at the present moment'. The print of Brunel standing before the launching chains of *The Great Eastern* seems to have been particularly popular and in the early 1860s the negative was acquired by the London Stereoscopic and Photographic Company with the intention of supplying prints to the public. However, the present print appears, from both its mount and its style of albumen printing, to have been produced around the time of the launch.

Far right:
Souvenir of Rejlander
Two plates from an
album of 32 photographs
by O.G. Rejlander
Albumen prints,
c. 1872-4
Each 8 × 6 in.
(20.2 × 15.2 cm)
Sold 15.3.79 for £4,000
($8,120)

Right
The Dream
By Julia Margaret
Cameron
Albumen print, 1869
12 × 9½ in.
(30.5 × 24 cm)
Sold 26.10.78 for £1,300
($2,600)

Fine Powell & Lealand 'Stand No. 1' binocular
and monocular microscope with accessories
1874
Sold 19.10.78 for £1,800 ($3,420)

Pair of steel-tipped brass calipers
By J. Sisson, London, mid-18th century
24½ in. (62 cm) long
Sold 8.2.79 for £950 ($1,900)

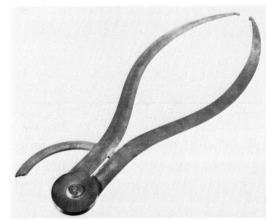

Reddings Luzo mahogany roll-film camera
Sold 30.11.78 for £1,000 ($1,900)

Fine Tropical Soho quarter-plate
reflex camera
Sold 22.3.79 for £1,500 ($3,000)

17.5 cm Ernemann Kino II
hand-cranked cine camera projector
Sold 17.5.79 for £550 ($1,100)

Fine English needlework picture
c. 1660
In 17th-century carved giltwood frame
12 ¾ × 16 ½ in. (32.3 × 42 cm)
Sold 15.5.79 for £5,000 ($10,000)

Fan
The guardstick set with a Celsius
thermometer
Inscribed: London 1778
11 in. (28 cm) long
Sold 17.7.79 for £760 ($1,672)

French suit of maroon
cut velvet
c. 1780
Sold 15.5.79 for £2,000
($4,000)

Far right:
Officer's levée coat of the
Surrey Yeomanry
c. 1800
Worn by Lord Leslie, later
George William, 13th Earl
of Rothes (1768-1817)
Sold 5.10.78 for £4,000
($7,600)

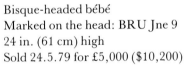

Bisque-headed bébé
Marked on the head: BRU Jne 9
24 in. (61 cm) high
Sold 24.5.79 for £5,000 ($10,200)

Heinrichsen 65mm Band of the Black
Watch in Review Order
Sold 8.2.79 for £200 ($400)

Fine set of crewelwork hangings
English, late 17th century (detail)
Sold 17.7.79 for £8,500 ($18,700)

Bisque shoulder-headed googly-eyed
doll
Marked: Einco 9 87.64 and with the
Heubach square mark
31 in. (78.8 cm) high
Sold 11.1.79 for £1,600 ($3,040)

Oh My
Printed tinplate clockwork
figure of a negro dancing
a jig
By Lehmann
10 in. (25.4 cm) high
Sold 18.1.79 for £230
($460)

German carpet toy train
set, 3½ in. gauge
Mid-19th century
Sold 19.7.79 for £800
($1,760)

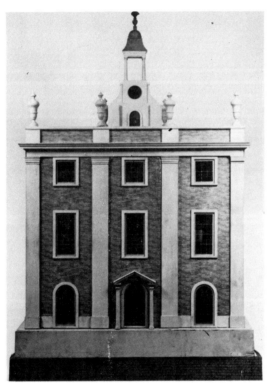

Doll's house designed by Sir Clough Williams
Ellis
40 in. (101.6 cm) high
The house is modelled on Orme Court where
Rupert Brooke was a frequent visitor: hence
the clock is set at ten to three
Sold 15.2.79 for £1,300 ($2,600)
Sold to the Portmeirion Trust

Selection from the sale of fountain pens and
the William Bishop Collection of writing
implements
Sold 1.3.79 for a total of £6,976 ($13,952)

Far left:
Fine Edison 'Red'
Gem phonograph
Sold 13.9.78 for £700
($1,330)
Record auction price
for this model

Fine Style No.6
Gramophone
By the Gramophone &
Typewriter Ltd.
1901
Sold 18.4.79 for £900
($1,800)
Record auction price
for a spring-driven
gramophone

Fine Stella 17¼ in. (44 cm) disc musical box in
inlaid mahogany case, *c.* 1900
44 in. (122 cm) high
Sold 13.9.78 for £1,900 ($3,610)

Fine 'Imperial' interchangeable cylinder
orchestral musical box
By Nicole Frères, *c.* 1900
48 in. (102 cm) wide
Sold 21.2.79 for £4,200 ($8,400)

A selection of tools from the
sale 23/24.4.79 of the stock of
Messrs Arnold & Walker
The sale, of 1,040 lots, totalled
£61,644 ($123,288)

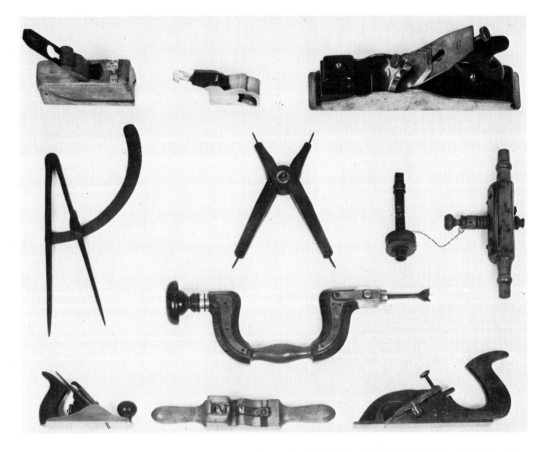

Fine Hall typewriter with
carrying case
c. 1885
Sold 8.2.79 for £320 ($640)

A.J.S. Type F6 four-valve
radio receiver, with Ethovox
horn speaker
Sold 8.11.78 for £420 ($840)

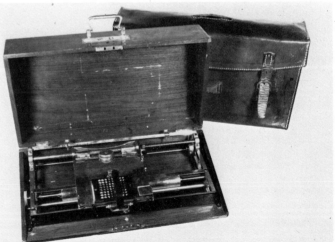

1954 Rolls-Royce
Silver Dawn foursome
drophead coupé
Coachwork by Park
Ward, London
Sold 24.4.79 in the
Netherlands for
D. fl. 72,000
(£17,266)

1919 Indian 994 c.c. Daytona twin racing motorcycle
Sold 9.7.79 at Beaulieu, Hampshire for £2,500 ($5,250)

1933 Packard Standard 8 series-1001
three-passenger convertible roadster
Sold 25.2.79 in Los Angeles, California for
$55,000 (£28,947)

1909 Reo Model-H Express truck
Sold 25.2.79 in Los Angeles, California for
$11,000 (£5,789)

1929 Mercedes-Benz **SS 38/250** h.p. two-passenger Sport Roadster
Coachwork by Corsica, **London**
Sold 25.2.79 in Los **Angeles, Cali**fornia for $320,000 (£168,421)
From the collection of **the late M.**L. 'Bud' Cohn

1936 Mercedes-Benz type **500K** two-passenger Roadster
Sold 25.2.79 in Los Angeles, **California** for $400,000 (£210,526)
From the collection of the **late M.L.** 'Bud' Cohn
Record auction price for **a motor-car**

Left to right:
Early 20th-century spirit-fired tinplate hot-air **engine set with** twin cylinders
14 × 12½ in. (35.5 × 32 cm)
Sold for **£220 ($440)**

20th-century overtype **live steam,** spirit-fired tinplate **stationary steam** set
By Doll et Cie
14 × 12½ in. (35.5 × 32 cm)
Sold for £260 ($520)

Early 20th-century live steam, spirit-**fired tinplate** stationary steam set
By Carette
17 × 10½ in. (43 × 26.5 cm)
Sold for £120 ($240)

All sold 30.4.79 at the Brighton and **Hove** Engineerium

Detailed 5 in. gauge model of the London and South Western
Railway Adams 4-4-0 locomotive and tender No. 575
Built by D.W. Horsfall, Halifax, 1966-74
15 × 58½ in. (38 × 148.5 cm)
Sold 30.4.79 at the Brighton and Hove Engineerium for £3,600
($7,200)

Exhibition standard 1/10 scale model of the famous 1924
8-litre 'Tulip Wood' Hispano Suiza, Reg. No. XX 3883
Built by Rex Hays
6 × 22 in. (15 × 56 cm)
Sold 30.4.79 at the Brighton and Hove Engineerium for £1,800
($3,600)

Fully rigged early 19th-century bone and horn model 30-gun frigate
17 × 29 ½ in. (53 × 75 cm)
Sold 30.4.79 at the Brighton and Hove Engineerium for £5,500 ($11,000)

Fully rigged French prisoner-of-war
boxwood, ebony and copper-sheathed
model of the 50-gun frigate 'La Gloire'
14 × 19½ in. (35.5 × 48 cm)
Sold 25.9.78 at the Brighton and Hove
Engineerium for £2,800 ($5,320)
From the collection of Lieutenant
Colonel C. Earle, DSO, OBE

¼ in. scale fully rigged dockyard model
of a sixth rate 24-gun man-of-war of
1684, built from the original drafts of
William Keltridge
By E.C. Freeston, Hailsham
28 × 31 in. (71 × 79 cm)
Sold 30.4.79 at the Brighton and Hove
Engineerium for £2,600 ($5,200)

Christie's Fine Arts Course

ROBERT CUMMING

From Japan to Venezuela, from Mexico to Canada, and from all over Europe, more than seventy students assembled at Christie's Fine Arts Course on the morning of 28 September 1978. In retrospect they admitted they gathered together with some trepidation — especially the older students who were risking going back to 'school' again — anxious to see who else had overcome the first hurdle of the interview, and positively alarmed when they discovered the amount of energy and dedication that Christie's expected from them. But they rose to the challenge, and before the end of the first term the intricate jigsaw puzzle of styles and influences, of furniture, ceramics, painting and sculpture, firearms, auction houses, catalogues, history, was beginning to take shape. By the end of June and the end of the Course the last pieces of the jigsaw were rapidly slotting in, and the happy faces and the volume of conversation in the coffee breaks told their own story: our students were returning home with regret that their year with Christie's Fine Arts Course was over, and that there was no second helping.

Christie's was founded in the age of the Grand Tour, and the saleroom has always retained that air of excitement and discovery in both objects and friendships that was part of 18th-century education. The opening of the railways and the growth of the ideas of industrialization spelled the end of the great Grand Tours (as well as of their discomfort), but the need for the sort of broadening of the horizon which the Grand Tour gave has never died. Thus it is particularly appropriate that Christie's can now encourage within its own domain an interest and knowledge in those works which have passed and do pass through its auction rooms, as well as give a basic training in those skills which anyone who wants to follow a career in the art world must have. It is not too extravagant to boast that our Fine Arts Course is, in part, the modern equivalent of the Grand Tour.

We hope that as well as establishing a reputation for making study a pleasure we have also founded our claim to provide an education and a training as good as that anywhere in the world. We have received enormous support and encouragement from scholars, collectors, dealers, museums and institutions all over this country and abroad, and to all of them we express our greatest thanks for the generosity with which they have shared their knowledge, their collections, their time and their enthusiasm. Our particular thanks go to Professors Francis Haskell, J. H. Plumb and Alan Bowness, who gave the Christie's Lectures for 1978/79 in aid of the National Art Collections Fund and the Contemporary Art Society.

We have set ourselves a high standard. The challenge is back with us.

WINE

Fine Wine Sales

MICHAEL BROADBENT

A BUOYANT MARKET

The 1978/9 season opened with a bang on 21 September with a 'Finest and Rarest' sale of the highest quality arranged to provide the focal point of the second, and highly successful, 'Concorde to Christie's' wine tour. The sale set the tone for an extremely active autumn — a pattern of sales very much along the lines firmly established from the moment wine sales at Christie's were resumed, after a break of a quarter of a century, in October 1966.

At that time, thirteen years ago, we were asked a question which has been repeated on many subsequent occasions: will the supply of old wines ever dry up? First of all, the better the prices we obtain for old wines, the more the sales receive publicity and the more bottles are willingly extracted from cellars where they would otherwise moulder; secondly, wines which were being vintaged the autumn we re-started are now a nicely-maturing thirteen years old, and a highly marketable commodity: 1966 château-bottled clarets in particular, but also 1966 burgundy and vintage port.

Prices throughout the season have been buoyant. The fine wine market has completely recovered from the slump of 1974/5 and the price increases which began in the autumn of 1976 and accelerated through 1977 and 1978 continued through to the spring of 1979, although in the most recent sales there has been a slight pause in the upward march in the price of first growth claret of classic vintages. Lesser growths have continued upwards; mature burgundy prices have been very strong in sympathy with the very high prices of young vintages in Burgundy itself. Immature vintage port (1970 and 1966 in particular) is undervalued and underpriced, but the demand for mature wines has been steady.

Rarities are always rarities and the demand is always ahead of the supply. Some of the highest prices of the 'finest and rarest' follow.

SPECIAL CHÂTEAU SALES

A special feature of this season's wine sales has been the highly successful sales featuring individual Bordeaux châteaux. The most important was the sale of a wide range of vintages from one of the most celebrated estates in Bordeaux: the Domaines Woltner.

The great respect in which Château La Mission Haut-Brion is held was amply borne out by the complete success of the sale of wines from the private cellars of the owners, the Woltner family, held at Christie's on Tuesday, 12 December.

At a very well attended evening sale, £88,266 ($174,767) was paid for 433 lots of wines from the family cellars: 62 vintages of Château La Mission itself from 1878 to 1975, 32 vintages of Château La Tour Haut-Brion from 1904 to 1975, and 46 vintages of dry white Laville Haut-Brion from 1928 to 1976. Of the 97 buyers, 38 were from overseas (taking 39% of the total

486

Above left:
Château Suduiraut

Above right:
Notre Dame de la Mission, consecrated in 1698, at Château La Mission Haut-Brion

sold); of these, 42% were American, the rest being from Australia, Germany, Holland, Switzerland and elsewhere.

All the wine on offer was sold, and the highest prices included:

£105 ($208) for a bottle of a century-old La Mission 1878
£24 ($47.50) for the first white wine ever made by the Domaine: the 1928 Laville

La Mission Haut-Brion 1929	£540 ($1,069) (double magnum)
La Mission Haut-Brion 1929	£820 ($1,624) per dozen bottles
La Mission Haut-Brion 1945	£500 ($990) per six bottles
La Mission Haut-Brion 1949	£550 ($1,089) (impériale)
Laville Haut-Brion 1945 (*crème de tête*)	£110 ($218) (bottle)

Cognac 1830
£85 ($184)

Tokay, believed 1649
£320 ($691)

Crême de Thé
£125 ($270)

Lacrima Christi
£42 ($90)

Cognac 1858
£68 ($146)

All sold 21.6.79 in
London

And of more recent vintages:

La Mission Haut-Brion 1961	£550 to £620 ($1,089 to $1,228) per dozen
La Mission Haut-Brion 1966	£200 to £210 ($396 to $416) per dozen
La Mission Haut-Brion 1967	£125 to £130 ($247 to $257) per dozen
La Mission Haut-Brion 1970	£170 to £175 ($337 to $346) per dozen
	£220 ($436) per six magnums
La Mission Haut-Brion 1971	£105 ($208) per dozen

The previous week we held our first special sauternes sale: 21 vintages of Château Suduiraut (1er cru classé, Preignac), including the pre-phylloxera wines and a half-bottle of the 1820, the oldest fully-authenticated sauternes sold at auction in recent years. The wine was offered in the third section of a magnificent sale of Finest and Rarest wines on 30 November.

In the spring, in a Claret and White Bordeaux sale, we offered an interesting range from an excellent but relatively little known premier cru from Saint-Emilion: Château Magdelaine.

All the above sales were supported by a fully illustrated catalogue with a history of each château and notes about the quality and style of the various vintages. The La Mission and the Magdelaine sales were also supported by illustrated articles and tasting notes in *Decanter* magazine. Indeed, we go as far as to say that such sales benefit all concerned. Our clients enjoy the unrivalled opportunity to taste and buy vintages normally unobtainable and from the most impeccable of sources; those catalogue subscribers who cannot attend the sale can at least read about the wines — and it is all excellent publicity for the châteaux and helps stimulate the trade in quality wines.

The combination of scale, style and coverage of the annual Heublein wine auction is impressive. From a modest beginning in 1969 the event has grown into what is undoubtedly the greatest annual wine event in the United States.

Held in different cities, this year's, on 24 May, was — for the fourth time — in Chicago. From the start it has been a combined operation, the entrepreneurial effort in this instance being American, with Christie's advising upon and conducting the sale in a properly English fashion: a highly successful Gilbert and Sullivan operation with Alexander C. McNally of the Wine Companies of Heublein Inc. assembling the wines and preparing the sumptuously printed catalogue, and myself, as head of Christie's Wine Department, taking the sale. Wide-ranging pre-sale tastings are held in other cities, McNally and Broadbent presiding over and commenting on samples of incredible rarities.

The 711-lot all-day sale achieved a total of $514,485 (£250,968), of which the star item was yet another bottle of the 1806 Lafite which sold, after feverish bidding, for $28,000 (£13,658), a world record price for any wine.

The autumn wine sale for Sakowitz in Houston was, as always, more modest and low-keyed, limited as it is to private residents of Texas. Nevertheless this relatively small sale was very well attended and the knock-down total was $65,000 (£32,500).

FINEST AND RAREST

This is the type of sale which Christie's is adept at handling. In it appears the *crème de tête* of the world's wines. There were three such sales during the season, two in the autumn and one in June. Here is a selection of the most notable wines and prices (dollar equivalents approximated at £1 = $2):

Red Bordeaux

1806	Ch. Lafite	£3,300 ($6,600) (bottle)
1854	Ch. Lafite	£1,000 ($2,000) (bottle)
1868	Ch. Lafite	£560 ($1,120) (bottle)
1868	Ch. Lafite (Berry Bros.)	£280 ($560) (bottle)
1869	Ch. Lafite	£1,050 ($2,100) (bottle)
1870	Ch. Lafite	£1,000 ($2,000) (magnum)
1872	Ch. Lafite	£310 ($620) (bottle)
1875	Ch. Lafite	£350 ($700) (bottle)
1877	Ch. Lafite	£370 ($740) (bottle)
1900	Ch. Lafite	£1,550 ($3,100) (magnum)
1945	Ch. Lafite	£1,900 ($3,800) per dozen
1949	Ch. Lafite	£740 ($1,480) per dozen
1924	Ch. Margaux	£800 ($1,600) (impériale)
1929	Ch. Margaux	£720 ($1,440) per nine bottles
1928	Ch. Latour	£560 ($1,120) per six bottles
1929	Ch. Latour	£420 ($840) (magnum)
1945	Ch. Latour	£1,150 ($2,300) per dozen
1949	Ch. Latour	£740 ($1,480) (magnum)
1900	Ch. Mouton-Rothschild	£520 ($1,040) (magnum)

Lund King's Screw with three steel springs to grip
the bottle
Marked: THE QUEENS PATENT GRANTED to
T. Lund (1838)
Sold 21.6.79 in London for £380 ($820)

1945	Ch. Mouton-Rothschild	£1,600 ($3,200) per dozen
1947	Ch. Mouton-Rothschild	£240 ($480) (magnum)
1949	Ch. Mouton-Rothschild	£960 ($1,920) per dozen
1947	Ch. Pétrus	£820 ($1,640) per six bottles
1961	Ch. Pétrus	£260 ($520) (magnum)
1947	Ch. Cheval-Blanc	£170 ($340) (magnum)

Sauternes

1820	Ch. Suduiraut	£500 ($1,000) (half-bottle)
1865	Ch. d'Yquem	£420 ($840) (bottle)
1869	Ch. d'Yquem	£480 ($960) (bottle)
1871	Ch. d'Yquem	£250 ($500) (bottle)
1900	Ch. d'Yquem	£400 ($800) (bottle)
1921	Ch. d'Yquem	£140 ($280) (bottle)
1929	Ch. d'Yquem	£160 ($320) (bottle)

Burgundy

| 1921 | Clos de la Roche | £52 ($104) (bottle) |
| 1959 | Grands Echézeaux (D.R.C.) | £380 ($760) per dozen |

Madeira

1715	Moscatel	£165 ($330) (bottle)
1789	Cama do Lobos	£220 ($440) (bottle)
1792	Blandy's	£180 ($360) (bottle)
1846	Terrantez	£140 ($280) (bottle)

Port

1834	Unknown shipper	£130 ($260) (magnum)
1847	Noval	£90 ($180) (bottle)
1955	Sandeman	£130 ($260) (tappit-hen)

Brandy

1805	La Tour d'Argent	£240 ($480) (bottle)
1811	Grande Armée	£440 ($880) (magnum)
1872	Janneau Armagnac	£165 ($330) (bottle)
1914	Croizet	£220 ($440) (magnum)
1921	Martell	£260 ($520) per three bottles

Tokay Essence (half-litres)

| 1649 | Imperial | £320 ($640) |
| 1888 | Essence | £155 ($310) |

Corkscrews

| Lund 1838 Patent | £380 ($760) |

Decanting cradles

| Victorian brass | £1,300 ($2,600) |

STAMPS

Stamps

In the past season a large number of finds have turned up and collectors have had the opportunity of competing for stamps and covers never previously on the market. The Great Britain market has been particularly strong: there have been no less than eleven specialized sales spread over fifteen days, total turnover more than £1,000,000. On 11 October the collection of the George V Sea-Horses types formed by the late R.M. Phillips of Brighton was sold on behalf of the Royal National Institute for the Blind, realizing an amazing total of £295,605 ($585,298). These issues have been very popular during recent years but there have been no collections of this size and stature on the market for twenty years and the 21 die proofs of one of the most popular designs ever prepared by Waterlow Brothers realized £88,000 ($172,480).

The greatest increase in value during the course of the season has been in the ever-popular, but quite common, penny blacks, the first adhesive postage stamps, issued on 6 May 1840. The value has risen by over 160% in the year and while there has been a large increase in the number of collectors and specialists in Great Britian there is no doubt that this stamp has attracted the attention of the investors. In the sale held on 5 and 6 December there were nearly a thousand penny blacks sold and prices for superb examples ranged from £150 ($297) to £900 ($1,782) a stamp. This interest has been spread over the later issues and one of the most surprising realizations was for a corner pair of the 1842 penny red-brown in fine used state (£1,600 ($3,168)).

The Mulready envelopes that were brought out at the same time as the penny blacks achieved new popularity. In February an example bearing an additional penny black went for £1,700 ($3,383) and another cancelled with a blue cross made £1,000 ($1,990), the same price being paid for a letter sheet posted on the first day of use, 6 May 1840. An envelope used on the same day made £2,000 ($3,960), while one which had been posted a day early (and for which the Post Office had charged a penny extra) made £4,250 ($8,458).

In March the King Edward VII section of the R. M. Phillips collection was sold and there were some quite startling results. A block of four of the 1902 2/6d made £2,600 ($5,304), a similar piece of the 5/- £3,400 ($6,936), while the three blocks of the 10/- went for £5,600 ($11,424), £5,000 ($10,200) and £4,600 ($9,384) respectively and a single copy of the £1 made £3,200 ($6,528). A mint corner block of the 1911 £1 made £11,500 ($23,460).

On 15 May the first part of a specialized collection of Mulready and illustrated envelopes formed by Wallace Knox of California came up for sale and there were many surprising prices. A used 2d letter sheet made £3,200 ($6,650) and a 1d envelope used on 4 May made £5,600 ($11,480), one posted on the following day realizing slightly less than half the figure, going for £2,700 ($5,535). A number of the caricatures realized over £1,000 ($2,050) each. The early

pictorial envelopes are attracting a lot of attention and one of the most handsome was the lady's envelope bearing a penny black posted from Dublin in October 1840 and illustrated on p.494; this started at £300 and finally changed hands at £1,300 ($2,665).

BERMUDA

Two sales were held in February. The first, British West Indies, realized a record total of U.S.$596,690 (£299,844). A set of eight 1844 colour trials for Antigua realized $9,000 (£4,502) and four colour trials for the 1907 issue of Caymans made $7,500 (£3,769). Among the stamps for this small colony a copy of the 5/- surcharged ½d in 1907 realized $8,000 (£4,020) because the surcharge had been carelessly struck twice.

The Leeward Islands as a group are well known but in 1890 consideration was given for a group issued inscribed Windward Islands. Fourteen key plate proofs were prepared for values from ½d to £1 but nothing ever came of the idea; the owner was pleased when this mythical issue realized $19,000 (£9,548).

BASLE

Twelve sales were held, four of which were held in October and realized Sw. fr. 1,630,183 (£539,796). In the Great Britain sale the unused 1840 penny and twopence made Sw. fr. 17,000 (£5,629) and one fine penny black made Sw. fr. 4,750 (£1,573). The highest price was Sw. fr. 30,000 (£9,934) for the unused mint block of four of the 1913 Waterlow £1.

The third sale dealt with Airmail stamps, the high spots being the French 1928 Ile de France provisionals, the unused pairs showing both spacings bringing Sw. fr. 25,000 (£8,278) and the inverted 10f./90c. Sw. fr. 8,500 (£2,815). Among the Swiss the 1935 inverted 10/15c. at Sw. fr. 12,000 (£3,974) and the mint 1938 Pro Aereo 75c./50c. at Sw. fr. 10,000 (£3,311) were bought by local collectors.

The fourth sale started off with the unused collection of the Koban issue of Japan made by the late Commander E. J. Allen; this small study fetched Sw. fr. 99,000 ($32,781). This was followed by the Arnold Waterfall collection of Tibet which made Sw. fr. 291,000 (£96,357); the 1903 cover from Khambajong with the typewritten overprint from a member of

Younghusband's expedition brought Sw. fr. 13,000 (£4,305). A 1923 envelope bearing two seals of the Dalai Lama sold for Sw. fr. 7,000 (£2,318) and a letter written by the Panchen Lama on the tail of his shirt brought Sw. fr. 11,000 (£3,642).

The eight sales held in Basle between 20 and 23 March realized Sw. fr. 1,500,000 (£428,571) and by now the pound had hardened to Sw. fr. 3.50. In the morning of the first day the room was well filled for the collection of Great Britain, the unused 1882 £5 making Sw. fr. 11,500 (£3,286) and many of the fine penny blacks fetching Sw. fr. 2,000 (£571) each or better. The Gibraltar 1889 missing value made Sw. fr. 10,000 (£2,857) and an envelope flown across the Atlantic by De Pinedo in 1927 brought Sw. fr. 12,500 (£3,571).

Next came a European sale in which the French section, which included the collection formed by the late H. V. Farmer, realized Sw. fr. 150,625 (£43,036). The German collections formed by Wing Commander W. L. Zigmond and the late Dr J. Schoenberger of New Zealand brought Sw. fr. 237,075 (£67,736). Italian, which included the collection of Lombardy Venetia formed by J. A. Foch of the Netherlands, brought Sw. fr. 256,175 (£73,193).

GENEVA

Two auctions were held in November in association with Christie's International S.A. Gibraltar started off the day, realizing Sw. fr. 121,780 (£37,820), the 1889 value omitted realizing Sw. fr. 8,500 (£2,640) and a corner pair Sw. fr. 15,000 (£4,658). A lightly mounted block of four of the 1928 £5 mint made Sw. fr. 16,000 (£4,969) and a used block Sw. fr. 17,250 (£5,357).

The companion collection of Malta brought Sw. fr. 169,620 (£52,677) and a mint block of ten of the 1860 ½d on blued paper made Sw. fr. 21,000 (£6,522), an imperforate corner block of four of the 1885 4d Sw. fr. 10,000 (£3,106) and the mint block of four of the 1919 10/- Sw. fr. 26,000 (£8,074).

The afternoon sale saw a fine collection of Russian Airmails which had been estimated at Sw. fr. 74,000 (£22,981), but soared to Sw. fr. 196,630 (£61,065).

Four sales were held in Geneva on 26 and 27 April and started off with British Empire rarities. A block of four of the Cyprus 1882 CA die I ½ piastre emerald made Sw. fr. 12,000

Western Australia 1854 4d with
inverted frame
Sold 27.4.79 in Geneva for
Sw. fr. 220,000 (£62,860)

(£3,429) and the Gibraltar 1889 missing value sold for a record price of Sw. fr. 18,000 (£5,145), more than the corner pair sold six months earlier. The only known example of the Iraq 1918 inverted 8 annas on 2½ pi. used made Sw. fr. 22,000 (£6,286) and the Trinidad Lady MacLeod 5c. on a letter sold for Sw. fr. 19,000 (£5,429). The latter part of the morning was devoted to Newfoundland Pioneer Airmails, many originally in the collection of the late Marquis of Bute. The Hawker 3c. mint went for Sw. fr. 18,000 (£5,143) and a copy on cover for Sw. fr. 21,000 (£6,000). The Martinsyde flight cover with the 3c. overprint in manuscript fetched Sw. fr. 58,000 (£16,570) and a mint example of the De Pinero 60c. made Sw. fr. 32,000 (£9,143), while the inverted D-OX surcharge made Sw. fr. 12,000 (£3,429) — the sale grossed Sw. fr. 477,928 (£136,551).

In the afternoon came the long-awaited collection of Western Australia formed by John Gartner of Melbourne. The first adhesive postage stamps were printed in London, the famous one penny black showing the black swan, and the star pieces were a mint block of eight which fetched Sw. fr. 29,000 (£8,286), a used block of six on envelope at Sw. fr. 46,000 (£13,143) and a rouletted pair on an envelope Sw. fr. 15,000 (£4,286).

Much of the interest lay in the major transfer varieties on the 4d locally lithographed, and the example with the inverted frame (above) fetched Sw. fr. 220,000 (£62,860), a record price many times over. This particular example had been bought just after the war for £300 and was sold by us some twenty years ago to John Gartner for £2,000. The PEICE variety made Sw. fr. 80,000 (£22,857), an unused block of 24 fetched Sw. fr. 65,000 (£18,571) and a pane of 60 made Sw. fr. 100,000 (£28,571).

In the De La Rue issues the 1864 double prints of the 4d made Sw. fr. 26,000 (£7,429) and Sw. fr. 24,000 (£6,857) for the two unused examples and the used 6d made Sw. fr. 38,000 (£10,857). Perhaps one of the most astounding prices was the Sw. fr. 18,000 (£5,140) paid for a triple surcharge of the 1875 ONE PENNY on 2d yellow, of which another example had sold for £700 in London earlier in the month.

The two days brought a total sale of Sw. fr. 1,969,520 (£562,720), the rate of the exchange at that time being £1 = Sw. fr. 3.50, U.S.$ = Sw. fr. 1.75.

There were fifteen sales held in London, the first being a section of a collection of South Australian Departmentals formed by the late Col. Harry Napier. This is a subject of very restriced philatelic interest but nevertheless there was keen competition. The Australian T.V. turned up and provided a new record inasmuch as the T.V. editor in Sydney who had bid on a lot had the doubtful pleasure of seeing the stamp on T.V. and listening to his bid failing.

One of the larger properties that contributed many fine stamps to the sales this season was the collection formed by the late Walter C. Hetherington,, whose British North America and British West Indies were sold in September and New South Wales in April. Other distinguished collections included the O. H. Downing Canada and the T. P. Palmer Falkland Islands which was sold on 12 October; the latter included an 1842 letter from a sailor written on board H.M.S. *Erebus* at Falkland Island with a vivid description of the local conditions and the wild life; this fetched £1,200 ($2,376). A small rectangular frank struck on an 1873 cover to Swansea fetched £3,250 ($6,435). The collection of essays and proofs for the King Edward VII issue was extremely popular and the 35 lots brought over £36,000 ($71,280). Some of the early covers from outlying islands did well, an 1899 cover from Fox Bay making £1,800 ($3,564), a 1909 envelope from New Island £2,300 ($4,554) and a 1910 cover from South Georgia £1,500 ($2,970).

On 21 December a fine collection of British West Africa formed by the late James Whitfield was sold. It included an 1883 envelope to London franked by half 6d and half 2d to make the 4d rate and this fetched £1,200 ($2,376). The same price was paid for a quartered 4d magenta used from Winnebah to Accra on an 1884 envelope.

The four London sales devoted to these stamps included many curious and exceptional lots. On 26 September a collection of forgeries formed by an American collector brought £8,500 ($16,660) and the very common Bavarian 1856 6 kr. used on the charming envelope illustrated on p. 493 made £475 ($931).

On 20 December a further portion of Col. John F. Rider's study of the Peruvian 1858 1 dinero came up under the hammer and a unique block cancelled TRUJILLO made £8,500 ($16,830), but even more surprising was an attractive registered cover bearing two singles which made £1,500 ($2,970).

Four of the most popular sales were held in Bournemouth and have the fortunate asset that they attract the real collectors and students rather than the curse of modern collecting, the investors. On 8 September a 1680 broadside advertising William Dockwara's London Penny Post brought £1,400 ($2,744); the collection of British Parcel Labels formed by the late J. A. O. Arkell brought £14,000 ($27,440).

On 1 December a 1687 entire letter to his daughters from Richard Cromwell and signed with his alias 'Crandberry' went for £520 ($1,030). A letter carried on Drummer's packet *ye Frankland* from Jamaica and addressed to London brought £950 ($1,881). Napoleon Buonaparte, when Artillery Commandant at Toulon in 1793 (he had just turned out the British), made £440 ($871). His opponent Horatio Nelson did better, for £700 ($1,386) each was paid for two letters, one written with his right hand to Lord Hood during the siege of Calvi in 1794 (the writer had lost an eye twelve days before), the other in 1803 with his left hand to 'My dear Emma . . . ever your most affectionate — ', left unsigned in case the letter was captured on its journey from the Mediterranean. A letter written on Christmas Eve 1839 bearing the handstamp 4 of Dorchester made £1,050 ($2,079).

In the March Postal History Auction a letter written in 1817 by a naval officer who was staying in St Helena with the Balcombes, whose little daughter Betsy was the exiled Napoleon's playmate, realized £1,600 ($3,264).

GENERAL SALES IN BOURNEMOUTH

A vital part of the business for twelve monthly sales saw fourteen tons of stamp collections sold for £1,423,813, bringing the total auction turnover for the year to £6,371,237 (1977-8 £4,093,620), an increase of 55%.

Christie, Manson & Woods, Ltd

LONDON
8 King Street, St. James's, sw1y 6qt
Telephone (01) 839 9060
Telegrams Christiart London sw1   *Telex* 916429
and 85 Old Brompton Road, sw7 3js
Telephone (01) 581 2231

GLASGOW
Christie's and Edmiston's Ltd
164-166 Bath Street, g2 4tg
Telephone (041) 332 8134

Agents in Great Britain and Ireland
ARGYLL
Sir Ilay Campbell, Bt.
Cumlodden Estate Office
Furnace by Inveraray, Argyll
Telephone (04995) 286

EDINBURGH
Michael Clayton
5 Wemyss Place, Edinburgh
Telephone: (031) 225 4757

NORTHUMBERLAND
Aidan Cuthbert
Eastfield House, Main Street
Corbridge, Northumberland
Telephone (043471) 3181

YORKSHIRE
Nicholas Brooksbank
46 Bootham, York   *Telephone* (0904) 30911

NORTH-WEST
Henry Bowring
Whelprigg, Kirkby Lonsdale
Cumbria   *Telephone* (046836) 337

WEST MIDLANDS
Michael Thompson
Stanley Hall, Bridgnorth
Shropshire   *Telephone* (07462) 61891

WEST COUNTRY
Richard de Pelet
Monmouth Lodge, Yenston
Templecombe, Somerset
Telephone (09637) 518

CORNWALL
Christopher Petherick
Tredeague, Porthpean
St. Austell, Cornwall   *Telephone* (0726) 64672

IRELAND
Desmond Fitz-Gerald, The Knight of Glin,
Private residence: 52 Waterloo Road, Dublin 2
Telephone (0001) 68 05 85
Office: Glin (068) 34173

NORTHERN IRELAND
John Lewis-Crosby
Marybrook House, Raleagh Road
Crossgar, Downpatrick, Co. Down
Telephone (0396) 830574

ISLE OF MAN
Quentin Agnew-Somerville
Mount Auldyn House, Ramsey
Isle of Man   *Telephone* (0624) 813724

CHANNEL ISLANDS
Richard de la Hey
8 St. David Place, St. Helier, Jersey
Telephone (0534) 77582

Companies and Agents Overseas
THE AMERICAS
United States
Christie, Manson & Woods International, Inc.,
502 Park Avenue, New York, N.Y. 10022
David Bathurst *President*
Telephone (212) 826 2888
Cables Chriswoods, New York
Telex (International) New York 620721
(Domestic) 710 5812325

Christie's East
219 East 67th Street
New York, N.Y. 10021
Telephone (212) 570 4141
Ray Perman

CALIFORNIA
Christie, Manson & Woods International, Inc.,
Suite 328, 9350 Wilshire Boulevard,
Beverly Hills, California 90212
Christine Eisenberg   Anne Johnson
Telephone (213) 275 5534   Michael Lampon
Telex 910 490 4652

PENNSYLVANIA
Mr. Paul Ingersoll
638 Morris Avenue, Bryn Mawr, Pa. 19010
Telephone (215) 525 5493

CHICAGO
Mrs. Edward McCormick Blair, Jr.
46 East Elm Street, Chicago, Illinois 60611
Telephone (312) 787 2765

Canada
Murray MacKay *Consultant*
Suite 2002, 1055 West Georgia Street,
Vancouver, British Columbia V6E 3P3
Telephone (604) 685 2126   *Telex* 04-507838

Mexico
Ana Maria de Icaza de Xirau *Consultant*
Callejon de San Antonio 64
San Angel, Mexico 20 D.F.
Telephone (905) 548 5946

Argentina
Cesar Feldman *Consultant*
Libertad 1269, 1012 Buenos Aires
Telephone 41 1616 or 42 2046
Cables Tweba, Buenos Aires

Australia
Sue Hewitt
298 New South Head Road
Double Bay, Sydney, 2028
Telephone 326 1422
Cables Christiart Sydney
Telex AA26343

Japan
Dodwell Marketing Consultants
No. 1 Kowa Building,
11-41 Akasaka, 1-chome,
Minato-ku, Tokyo 107.
Telephone (03) 584 3251   *Telex* J22274
Kunio Oshima

EUROPE
Austria
Vincent Windisch-Graetz
Ziehrerplatz 4/22
1030 Vienna   *Telephone* 73 26 44

Belgium
Christie, Manson & Woods (Belgium) Ltd.
33 Boulevard de Waterloo
1000 Brussels
Richard Stern
Telephone 512 8765 or 8830
Telex Brussels 62042

France
Christie's (France) SARL
68 rue de l'Université, 75007 Paris
Princesse Jeanne-Marie de Broglie
Telephone 544 16 30   *Telex* Paris 200024

Le Marquis d'Oyley
Le Pailler
rue la Fontaine
06550 La Roquette-sur-Siagne
Alpes Maritimes
Telephone (93) 75 67 68

Italy
Christie's (International) S.A.
Palazzo Massimo Lancellotti
Piazza Navona 114, Rome 00186
Telephone 654 1217   *Telex* Rome 62524
Marchese dott. Paolo del Pennino
d.ssa. Luisa Vertova Nicolson *Consultant*

Sandro Perrone di San Martino
Corso Vittorio 86, 10121 Turin
Telephone 011 548819

Christie's (Italy) S.r.l.
9 via Borgogna
20144 Milan   *Telephone* 794 712
Edoarda Sanna

Norway
Ulla Klaveness
Vestre Kjøyavejen 12
1324 Lysaker
Telephone (Oslo) 122997

Spain
Casilda Fz.-Villaverde de Eraso
Carlos Porras
Edificio Propac
Casado del Alisal 5, Madrid 14
Telephone 228 39 00
Cables Christiart, Madrid *Telex* 43889

Sweden
Mrs. Lillemor Malmström
Hildingavägen 19
182 62 Djursholm, Stockholm
Telephone 755 10 92 *Telex* Stockholm 12916

Switzerland
Christie's (International) S.A.
8 Place de la Taconnerie, 1204 Geneva
Dr. Geza von Habsburg
Telephone 28 25 44   *Cables* Chrisauction Geneva
Telex Geneva 23634

Christie's (International) A.G.
Steinwiesplatz
8032 Zürich   *Telephone* 69 05 05
Maria Reinshagen

The Netherlands
Christie, Manson &'Woods Ltd.
Rokin 91, 1012 KL Amsterdam
Drs. Andries Baart
Telephone 231 505
Cables Christiart Amsterdam
Telex Amsterdam 15758

West Germany
Jörg-Michael Bertz
Alt Pempelfort 11a
4000 Düsseldorf
Telephone 35 05 77
Cables Chriskunst Düsseldorf
Telex 8587599

Max Graf Arco
Maximilianstrasse 20, 8000 Munich 22
Telephone 22 95 39

Charlotte Fürstin zu Hohenlohe-Langenburg,
Schloss Langenburg,
7183 Langenburg,
Württemberg
Telephone (7905) 241/2

Mrs Isabella von Bethmann Hollweg,
2331 Altenhof bei Eckernförde,
Telephone (4351) 41890

Acknowledgements

Christie's are indebted to the following who have allowed their names to be published as purchasers of works of art illustrated on the preceding pages. The figures refer to the page numbers on which the illustrations appear.

Gemaeldegalerie Abels, 132
Arthur Ackermann & Son Ltd, 54, 61
Acquavella Contemporary Art, Inc., 160
Alice Adam, Ltd, 119 (top left)
Thomas Agnew & Sons Ltd, 59, 107, 130
Albany Gallery, 103 (all)
Alexander Gallery, 37
Mr Michael Alishan, 402 (right)
Antique Porcelain Co., 342
Stad Antwerpen, 38
Artemis Group, 113, 115 (bottom)

Barbier-Müller Collection, Geneva, 414 (bottom right)
Mr R. F. Basil, 249
Baskett & Day, 56, 94 (top), 96 (top), 97 (bottom), 346 (bottom right)
Major D. R. Baxter, 436 (bottom left)
Mr Kaare Berntsen, 142
Mr Fritz Biemann, 351 (right)
H. Blairman & Sons Ltd, 206
Brisigotti Antiques, 219
Brod Gallery, 40, 45
Miss Y. Tan Bunzl, 128
D. Burgess, Esq., 218

Carson, Booth Antiques, 275 (top ring)
Edward Carter, 352 (centre)
C.D.P., Brussels, 34, 418
Charles Cheriff Galleries, 358 (top left)
Chess Gallery, 315 (top)
J. Cooper, Esq., 53, 55 (both)
Richard Courtnay Ltd, 202
Mr H. M. Cramer, 42

Miss Jacqueline Deatherage, 125 (top)
Delomosne & Son Ltd, 328 (top)
Mr David Drager, 307 (top)

Eskenazi Ltd, 371
Mr George Evens, 96 (bottom)

Al Fahrannick, 398
Jocelyn Feilding Fine Art Ltd, 43
The Fine Art Society Ltd, 108 (bottom right), 164 (top), 168, 174, 175
The Fine Arts Committee of the Department of State for the Diplomatic Reception Rooms, Washington D.C., 87 (bottom left and right), 211
Mr D. A. Finestein, Studio Anne Carlton Ltd, 315 (bottom)
Mr Isi Fischzang, 307 (centre right)
John Fleming, 179, 186
Victor Franses Gallery, 225
Fujii Gallery, 143

William E. Garlick, 240 (top)
Michael C. German, 432 (top), 436 (top)
Thomas Gibson Fine Art, 52
Judy and Alan Goffman Fine Art, 176 (right)
Lucien Goldschmidt, 118 (top left)
Graff Diamonds, 252 (bottom), 264 (left), 274 (lorgnette, bracelet)
Richard Green, 39, 44, 47, 51, 73 (top), 75 (top), 77, 82, 83, 109 (both), 127 (bottom left), 170 (top), 438 (bottom)
Martyn Gregory, 98
Ray and Lee Grover, 350 (right)

Stephen Hahn, 141
Professor E. T. Hall, 248
F. Hammond, Esq., 187, 193
Hancocks & Co., 272 (bottom)
S. H. Harris & Son (London) Ltd, 273 (ring at bottom right)
Hazlitt, Gooden & Fox, 127 (top)
Michael Hogg, 201
Hom Gallery, 123 (right)
How of Edinburgh, 280
John Howell Books, 184, 185
C. Humphris Ltd, 334, 336, 337
Mr Bernard Hurtig, 7

H. R. Jessop Ltd, 283

Mr Y. W. Kadri, 316 (left top and bottom)
Mr Leo Kaplan, 314 (both)
Khalili Gallery, 399 (top)
Clifford E. King, 192
David Koetser Gallery, 32
E. & C. T. Koopman & Son Ltd, 284, 285, 286 (centre vases), 304 (bottom right)
Kunstanstalt Ex Oriente, 316 (top right)

Mr C. C. Lai, 368
D. S. Lavender, 302 (centre right), 306 (top)
P. Lazarus, 350 (top left)
Mr K. H. Lee, 394 (left)
Leggatt Bros, 50, 169, 303 (left)
Collection of Sydney and Frances Lewis, 159, 266 (left)
Collection of the Sydney and Frances Lewis Foundation, 359 (right)
Simon Lieberman Ltd, 360
Limner Antiques, 303 (top right)
N. W. Lott & H. J. Gerrish Ltd, 126 (top)

J. S. Maas & Co. Ltd, 64, 67, 108 (top)
Macmillan & Perrin Gallery, 166
Maggs Bros Ltd, 195
Mansour Gallery, 397, 399 (bottom left)
Hans Marcus, 127 (bottom right)
Matsuoka Museum of Art, 2, 364 (left, centre), 366 (bottom)

C. Mendez, 111 (top left)
Roy Miles Fine Paintings, 73 (bottom), 75 (bottom)
John Mitchell & Son, 46, 101
Mizes & Mizes, 258
Musée d'Art et d'Histoire, Geneva, 48 (both)
G. Music & Son Ltd, 275 (necklace)

Mr H. R. Nasser, 411
National Gallery of Ireland, 57
Albrecht Neuhaus, 220, 236
David Newbon, 331
Noble Antiques, 388 (top right)

Anthony d'Offay, 165, 167

Partridge Fine Art, 244
S. J. Phillips Ltd, 256 (pearl brooch), 292, 306 (bottom), 307 (all except top and centre right), 310
Count Pignatelli, 204
Mr Hermann Plenge Antiquair, 439 (top left)
Michel Postel, 402 (left)

B. Quaritch Ltd, 181, 191

Mr Alan Hartman, Rare Art Inc., 373
Heinz Reichert, 341 (right)
Mr C. Roobol-Fritz, 441 (right)
Mr Trevor Rostron, 188, 190

Kurt E. Schon Ltd, 60
Mr Martin Selig, 161
Dr Helmut W. Seling, 295
S. J. Shrubsole Ltd, 281, 286 (candlesticks)
Société des Manuscrits et Autographes Français, 194
Mr S. Spero, 330 (top right)
Spink & Son Ltd, 58, 164 (bottom), 170 (bottom), 171, 352 (top right, bottom left), 388 (top centre)
Alice F. Steiner, 94 (bottom)
Mr E. Stender, 247
Mr Philip A. Straus, 123 (left)
Oliver Sutton Antiques, 329
Mr Janos Szekeres, 364 (right)

Mr Taylor, 183
Tempus Antiques Ltd, 388 (bottom left)
B. & T. Thorn, 328 (bottom left)
Dr A. Torré. 341 (left), 347 (right top and bottom)
David Tunick Inc., 116 (bottom)

Van Doren Gallery, 317
Victoria & Albert Museum, 278 (top right)
Mr H. L. Visser, 431, 433, 436 (second from top)
Jordan Volpe Gallery, 87 (top)

The David Warner Foundation, 88
Mr Waroujian, 396

Wartski, 312 (left top and bottom)
B. Warwick, 377 (both), 379, 380
Wellington Antiques, 210
Mr H. Wernick, 65
R. J. Wigington, Esq., 436 (centre left)
Winifred Williams, 326, 330 (top left), 346 (top, bottom left), 347 (bottom left)
Williams and Son, 86
Christopher Wood, 69
Mr Martin Wright, 415
Andrew Wyld, Esq., 104 (bottom)

J. &. S. S. de Young, Inc., 252 (centre)

Index

Index

There was an Old Man of Whitehaven, who danced a quadrille with a Raven;
But they said—"It's absurd, to encourage this bird!"
So they smashed that Old Man of Whitehaven.

That was a Young Lady of Bute, who played on a silver-gilt flute;
She played several jigs to her uncles white pigs,
That amusing young Lady of Bute.